First Unit Responder

A Guide to Physical Evidence Collection for Patrol Officers

Mark R. Hawthorne

CRC Press
Boca Raton   London   New York   Washington, D.C.

Acquiring Editors:	H. Kane
Project Editor:	Sylvia Wood
Marketing Manager:	Becky McEldowney
Cover design:	Dawn Boyd

Library of Congress Cataloging-in-Publication Data

Hawthorne, Mark R.
    First unit responder : a guide to physical evidence collection for
    patrol officers / Mark R. Hawthorne
            p.   cm.
        Includes bibliographical references and index.
        ISBN 0-8493-0023-1 (alk. paper)
        1. Criminal investigation--Handbooks, manuals, etc. 2. Crime
    scene searches--Handbooks, manuals, etc. 3. Evidence, Criminal-
    -Handbooks, manuals, etc. 4. Evidence preservation--Handbooks,
    manuals, etc. I. Title.
    HV7936.E85H39 1998
    363.25'2—dc21
    for Library of Congress

                                                            98-33534
                                                                CIP

DEDICATION

This book is dedicated to two people who have nurtured me in my personal and professional life over the past 25 years They are my wife, Sheila, who has blessed me with two beautiful children and an understanding relationship that has allowed me to grow as a person; and Ken Moses, who provided the opportunity in 1984 for me to enter the Crime Scene Investigations Unit and begin my career as a professional in the field of Forensic Identification.

Both Sheila and Ken have impacted my life substantially, albeit in different arenas.

To both, I wish to say thank you for the opportunities and special moments.

Wherever he steps, whatever he touches, whatever he leaves, even unconsciously, will serve as silent evidence against him. Not only his fingerprints or his footprints, but his hair, the fibers from his clothing, the glass he breaks, the toolmark he leaves, the paint he scratches, the blood or semen that he deposits or collects—all these and more bear mute witness against him. This is evidence that does not forget. It is not confused by the excitement of the moment. It is not absent because human witnesses are. It is factual evidence. Physical evidence cannot be wrong; it cannot perjure itself; it cannot be wholly absent. Only its interpretation can err. Only human failure to find it, study and understand it, can diminish its value.

Presiding Judge
Harris v U.S., **331 U.S. 145 (1947)**

Preface

The significance of proper identification, care, and booking of physical evidence in criminal cases cannot be taken lightly. In many instances, the physical evidence is the only manner in which a crime can be proven, or that a particular suspect, in fact, committed the crime. Inappropriate or poor training techniques lead to poor practices when coming in contact with physical evidence or maintaining the integrity of the crime scene. In court, the integrity of the evidence can easily be challenged by the defense, which can result in dismissal of the charges, or the finding of a lesser offense against the criminal defendant. This action can easily be avoided by providing proper training and guidance to first unit responders as part of their core curriculum of study in the training academy.

In my 14 years as a Crime Scene Investigator and Instructor at Community Colleges and at the Police Academy, I have not seen a text devoted strictly to training the first unit responder in the detection, identification, preservation, handling, and booking of physical evidence. Numerous texts have been written on the subject of physical evidence and the many facets of physical evidence when part of a larger criminal investigation, as it relates to the follow-up investigation by detectives. In writing this book I have attempted to create a publication that will serve as a guideline for all first unit responders, i.e., patrol personnel who respond to crime scenes, identify, collect, and book physical evidence. This book is meant to be a useful tool for police academies that train recruit and veteran patrol officers, as well as to the student of criminal justice seeking a training text on the subject of identifying, handling, processing, and booking physical evidence. This book is not designed to be an extremely in-depth or complex text covering the subject of physical evidence, but rather a straightforward publication to assist the patrol officer and, in some instances, the new investigator or detective in handling a case. Its essence is to stress how essential it is to understand the critical nature of physical evidence as part of the case against a criminal defendant.

Introduction

Patrol officers responding to scenes of crimes are delegated a great deal of responsibility. At the same time, crime scenes can be very chaotic during the early moments following the arrival of the police. To keep chaos from being destructive to the case and the crime scene, proper training and reinforcement are vital if police are expected to maintain professional calm in the face of adversity, yet still retain the integrity of the scene, and the evidence, as well as provide aid to those who have been injured as a result of the crime.

The first unit responder must be prepared, in many instances, to make split-second decisions on arrival to a reported crime. These decisions can have a lasting impact on victims, witnesses, the accusatory process, and even the community in which the crime occurred. There is no greater reward for a police officer than to catch a criminal in the commission of a crime. Realistically, and all too often, the patrol officer will arrive after the criminal act has taken place. Left in the wake of the crime, police officers are confronted with the victims, witnesses, and physical evidence.

As a veteran of 25 years of law enforcement, I am all too familiar with criminal cases where police officers were careless and valuable evidence was not identified, not collected, or lost, resulting in a poor follow-up by investigating officers or detectives. Worse yet, this carelessness has, in some situations, lost the only evidence with which to prove or disprove that a crime was committed and identify who the perpetrator might have been. The critical nature of evidence cannot be discarded. Sometimes, the evidence is not easy to detect, preserve, or collect. Nonetheless, it is the responsibility of first unit responders to do their very best in conducting a preliminary investigation of a crime and the crime scene. In many instances, the responsibilities of first unit responders while at the scene are unclear or complicated. The depth and scope of the investigation is limited to what has been taught or what the office has been told to do as a common practice. The problem arises when police agencies are not operating under the same basic guidelines or principles required to properly handle physical evidence.

We are entering the 21st century, and the abilities and knowledge of the first unit responder must keep pace with new developments in the field of forensic identification. As sophisticated as the forensic identification unit within a department might be, and regardless of the advanced technology available, if the evidence to be analyzed is not identified or preserved, that analysis cannot be undertaken. It is a joint effort on the part of all personnel involved in the investigation process to ensure that the case will come to a successful conclusion.

This book was written for just such an application: for the first unit responder to use as a training guide and reference material. Its text offers definitions and procedures the first unit responder can apply when responding to a crime scene or handling physical evidence. It is written in an easy-to-understand format with definitions, examples, and test questions that will serve to simplify implementing procedures. This text is a must for training first unit responders in the identification and collection of physical evidence, and the preservation of the crime scene.

About the Author

Mark Hawthorne is a 25-year veteran of law enforcement. He has worked for the San Francisco Sheriff's Office and, for the past 18 years, has been employed by the San Francisco Police Department. He has served in a variety of assignments from uniform patrol to specialized units such as SWAT to that of a Field Training Officer. He earned a Bachelor of Arts degree in Administration of Justice from Golden Gate University and an Associate degree in Criminology from City College of San Francisco. He is a Certified Senior Crime Scene Analyst, a Certified Latent Print Examiner, an Instructor at City College of San Francisco in Administration of Justice, and is the Lead Instructor in Investigations at the San Francisco Police Academy. He has spent the last 14 years of his career in law enforcement working in Crime Scene Investigations unit, during which time he has attended hundreds of hours of forensic identification training, processed thousands of crime scenes, compared thousands of latent fingerprints, and has effected hundreds of identifications. He also has qualified as an expert witness in San Francisco Superior and Municipal courts, and the U.S. Federal Court in the area of identification, collection, preservation, and processing of physical evidence. He is also past-President of the California State Division, International Association for Identification, and is currently pursuing a Master's degree in Public Administration at Golden Gate University.

Contents

chapter one

The role of
the first unit responder

The patrol officer in law enforcement today is placed in a role with a variety of tasks and duties to perform. To the uninformed, the role might appear to be one of simplicity—that of patrolling the streets, ever vigilant for the presence of a criminal act, a violation against public peace, or being available as a resource. It has long been an unwritten rule for society that whenever something happens and there is no one else to turn to, call the police because they are trained to know what to do. Generally speaking, the police are going to be the first contact the public at large has with the Criminal Justice system. Unfortunately, those encounters, more often than not, are of the negative type, such as being a victim or a suspect in a crime. As with all facets of law enforcement, the patrol officer is expected to handle the situation professionally, conducting a preliminary investigation to determine if, in fact, a crime was committed. This undertaking is not always as clear-cut and easy as one might assume. Should the officer establish a crime was committed, the officer must then determine if there is a crime scene to document, if there is physical evidence related to the crime, if medical treatment is required, and must provide that needed medical assistance, attempt to locate additional victims or witnesses, and make proper notifications to supervisors and detectives should the situation warrant such action. To many veteran law enforcement officers, establishing the elements of the crime and identifying witnesses and/or additional victims is almost second nature. What does not appear to be second nature to many officers is the ability to properly identify the perimeter of a crime scene and, within that area, or possibly at a secondary scene, physical evidence that is connected to the criminal act. Throughout this chapter, and throughout the book, the significance of identifying, preserving, and collecting physical evidence will be discussed.

1.1 Importance of physical evidence

Why is it so important to identify and properly preserve physical evidence, one might ask? In certain instances, a cursory search can reveal to the first unit responding what type of weapon was used based up the type of casings left at the scene; in which direction the suspect(s) might have fled based on blood cast off or shoe impressions; or if a vehicle was used, as evidenced by tire impressions. All of this physical evidence can be extremely important, not only to the first unit, but to those who will be undertaking the follow-up investigation, e.g., detectives, crime scene units, or photo labs. Sound investigations, like anything else in life, begin with a good foundation. Every criminal case must have a foundation that is based upon facts that can later be proven. If the evidence is not located or properly preserved, the entire case may be in jeopardy. Often, identifying physical evidence is not an easy task, as the evidence can be very small and extremely fragile. Examples of this type of evidence might be in the form of hairs, fibers, paint chips, and / or fingerprints. Generally speaking, the more fragile the evidence, the greater the likelihood of that evidence being overlooked or destroyed. What does this mean in practical terms? A good first-year law student or rookie cop can tell you that when evidence of a crime cannot be produced, the case will probably be dismissed (a nice way of saying "thrown out").

In my research, I have found a term that amply describes the importance of building a proper case against a criminal defendant. **Section 871 of the California Penal Code** states: "If after hearing the proofs, it appears either that no public offense has been committed or that there is not sufficient cause to believe the defendant guilty of a public offense, the magistrate shall order the complaint dismissed and the defendant to be discharged ..." So, to say or imply that physical evidence in a case is less than important is to circum-vent the duties and responsibility a law enforcement officer is sworn to uphold. There are countless examples of cases in which the evidence was not properly collected and preserved. The most noted of such cases has been the one that received the most notoriety in recent years, the case against O.J. Simpson. Not wishing to bore anyone by reviewing the case step by step, let it suffice to say that, because of who the defendant was, the publicity surrounding the case, and the ultimate punishment that could have been inflicted, the case was scrutinized as minutely as a cell under a microscope. Mistakes were made regarding the physical-evidence handling, collection, and packaging, accounting in part for the acquittal of the defendant. This case sent a message to all law enforcement officials to take note of the importance of physical evidence, its identification, collection, and preserva-tion—a message that I feel was well received throughout the country as many agencies began looking at and upgrading their training to ensure that another incident of such magnitude would not happen at their agency. Administrators, as well as those practicing in the field of forensic identifica-tion have an obligation from time to time to review guidelines and policies and revise those documents as necessary to ensure that what is being done and how it is being done is as professional as possible.

1.2 Defining physical evidence

It is appropriate to begin by looking specifically at what is meant by physical evidence. How do we define what is being sought? What exactly is **physical evidence? It is anything that has been used, left, removed, altered, or contaminated during the commission of the crime, by either the victim(s) or suspect(s).** As the definition implies, physical evidence can be anything that might include something so insignificant as a pencil or even a paper clip, to the more complex such as a computer, or, what first enters the mind when one thinks of violent crimes, the all-too-familiar firearm. Just as public offenses or crimes run the gamut, so too does the evidence associated with those crimes. The key for the first unit responder is to first determine what type of crime was committed, and then attempt to identify the appropriate evidence associated with that crime. The first unit responder should bear in mind that he/she should not maintain the posture that many law enforcement officers are guilty of: that of being prosecution oriented. Law enforcement officers must continually remind themselves they have the duty to exonerate those not involved in the crime as well as implicating those who are responsible. Why is it so important to keep this idea in mind? For the simple reason that evidence can establish several things. For example, physical evidence:

- Cannot lie, forget, or be mistaken when properly identified and collected
- Is demonstrable
- Is not dependent on the presence of witnesses
- Is, in some instances, the only way to establish the elements of the crime

Look at each element associated with physical evidence and how it applies. The first—**cannot lie, forget, or be mistaken**— simply means that inanimate objects are not subject to human frailties—human emotions, prejudices, opinions, or greed. The key portion of the statement is **when properly identified and collected**. For example, if a screwdriver or some other type of pry tool that was recovered in a burglary case was not properly packaged, and the configuration of the tool changed, a match to the striation on a striker plate would not match the tool. Similarly, if a firearm were to be picked up by shoving a hard object down the barrel, the striation of the barrel might not match the striation of a bullet recovered from a gunshot victim. There are many other examples, but the point is clear: if the evidence is contaminated, it will be of little value in establishing certain facts of the case.

The next element—**demonstrable**—simply means that the evidence can be used to reconstruct what happened and possibly how it happened, a series of events. Simply, a demonstration can be undertaken in front of the trier of fact. The third—**not dependent on the presence of witnesses**—simply means that, in some instances, the evidence in and of itself can stand alone. For example, fingerprints found inside a residence in which the suspect had no right to be conclusively proves the suspect was there and probably committed the act. Another example, more common than one would like to think, occurs in hit-and-run accidents where there are no witnesses and the victim does not recall particular facts of the event. By simply comparing evidence such as paint transfer or pattern transfer, glass fragments found on the victim, or blood on a vehicle, one can establish conclusively that a certain vehicle was involved in the hit and run. The final element: **it is the only way to establish the elements of some crimes.** Looking back at the previous example of the burglary, one can take it a step further and say that the suspect was found at his home with a stolen stereo but denies it is his or that he touched it. Fingerprints would be the only way to establish that the suspect had, in fact, had the stereo in his possession. Another example might be to look at a sex crime, specifically rape. Analyzing the fluid from a vaginal swab can establish conclusively that the suspect did in fact commit the rape—especially in light of DNA analysis and although the suspect vehemently denies his guilt. The examples could go on indefinitely, but the point is well made about the usefulness of the physical evidence.

1.3 Characteristics of physical evidence

As has been alluded to previously, the type of physical evidence and its usefulness in the criminal investigation and subsequent prosecution is directly related to how the evidence is identified, preserved, and collected. This is important to note because, as strange as it sounds, some evidence can be much more damaging than other evidence. To the untrained person, the idea of evidence is simply that: evidence. Many times, there is no differentiation made between the types of evidence gathered in a criminal case or its relevance. For example, the type of evidence that can be shown to match a particular item or person to the exclusion of all others is much more damaging than evidence that is similar to, or consistent with, a particular person or thing. Being able to place the evidence in one of the two categories is very important because it underlines the strength or weight of the evidence in the overall presentation of the case.

The two categories or types of characteristics that all physical evidence will fall into is either **Individual Characteristic or Class Characteristic.**

What distinguishes the two types of evidence listed above? The first type, **individual characteristic**, refers to **a piece of evidence that is unique and can be identified to the exclusion of all others**. Its uniqueness is created through unintentional alteration or wear, or based on the uniqueness at the time of creation, or based on biological variation that allows the evidence to be introduced as individual or unique to the exclusion of all others. An example of this is something that is almost universally accepted: the human fingerprint. All human beings have fingerprints and all of those fingerprints fall into one of three types of patterns: arches, loops, or whorls (Figure 1.1).

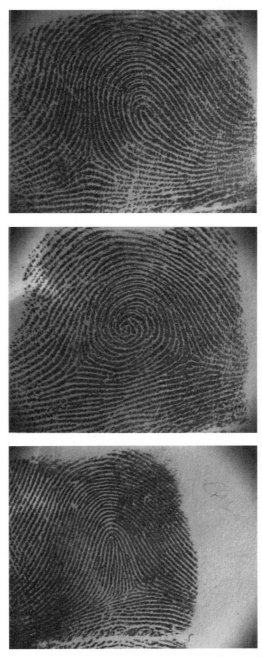

Figure 1.1 - Examples of the three types of fingerprints. What makes each unique is the location and type of ridge characteristics contained within the fingerprint patterns. Fingerprints share both class and individual classification characteristics.

Not everyone has all three of these types of patterns, but many people may have similar patterns in terms of size and shape. This would be an example of **class characteristics**, or **features shared by all members of a group or class** (see Figure 1.2). However, that is where the similarities end. Within the pattern, there are ridge characteristics that are unique to that particular pattern and no other. It is from the uniqueness of the ridge characteristics (the appearance of certain types of ridge characteristics and their relative position in the known and latent) that allow for an identification of the fingerprint to the exclusion of all others. Another example of individual characteristic evidence might be a bullet recovered from a crime scene (an unknown). Should a weapon be later recovered, a test shot can be fired (a known). The two bullets can subsequently be compared through a microscope to determine if they match to the exclusion of all others. If the striation on both the known and the unknown bullets match, individual characteristics have been established. As one can see, the enormity of individual characteristic evidence is much greater than that of class characteristic evidence.

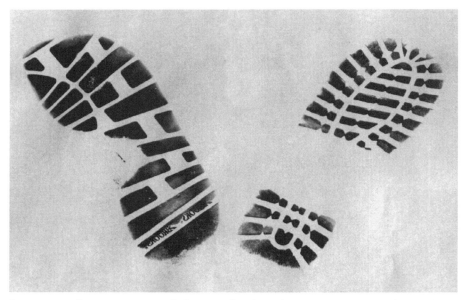

Figure 1.2 - Shoe impressions belong in the class characteristic until individualized characteristics can be identified and compared with a known impression or the shoe itself.

Although not as damaging as individual characteristic evidence, class characteristic is also important as a form of evidence. Physical evidence of class type, also known as circumstantial evidence, can be devastating when presented under the right circumstances. If enough class evidence is recovered, the likelihood of all of the evidence appearing at a certain place, at a certain time, can have an impact on the weight of the evidence and on the jury. Keeping this in mind, one can see how important it is for the first unit responder to properly identify, preserve, and/or collect the physical evidence at the crime scene so that later analysis can be successfully undertaken. Should the first unit responder overlook, contaminate, or alter the physical evidence when responding to, or conducting, the crime scene search, the evidence might not be rendered unusable, but the degree to which the evidence will be able to show with certainty what occurred might be altered. That is not to say that evidence at crime scenes will not be contaminated or altered accidentally due to the critical nature of some scenes and incidents; but to the extent that first unit responders can do everything within their power to maintain the integrity of the evidence and the scene, they must do so. One must be realistic enough to realize that there will be situations where the evidence will be altered or even destroyed and we accept that as part of the incident. This is termed a *mechanical loss*, for lack of a better term. An example of this would be where there is evidence next to a gunshot victim and the paramedics rush in, attempting to save a life, and alter or destroy the evidence. Unfortunately, this is a fact of life that must be accepted—for it is better to save a life and lose the evidence, than to lose the life and maintain the integrity of the evidence. By the same token, if the first unit responder can clear a pathway for the responding emergency medical units, which means moving or traveling around the evidence, then discretion might be the better part of valor. (The evidence should be moved to prevent loss or contamination.)

This chapter has covered some basic concepts as to why it is necessary to clearly identify if a crime was committed, if there is physical evidence and/or a crime scene, why the scene and the evidence must be protected, and how strong is the evidence recovered. The rookie cop or the experienced veteran need to review, from time to time, how to perform their duties and critique themselves on their performance. Should they fail to do something so simple as a periodic review of what they do and how they do it, they are of little real value to the agency that employs them and the community they are sworn to protect.

1.4   Review

Criminal cases are often dismissed by the magistrate due to the lack of proof that a public offense was committed, and that a defendant committed said offense. Physical evidence is just as important, if not more important, than other types of testimonial evidence because:

- It does not lie, forget, or make mistakes when properly collected.
- It is demonstrable.
- It is not dependent on the presence of witnesses.
- In some situations, it is the only way to establish the elements of the crime or the identity of the criminal suspect.

Physical evidence will be of two types: **Individual and Class Characteristic**. Generally speaking, the more individualized the evidence, the more fragile it will be.

Contamination and destruction of the physical evidence and the crime scene is acceptable in some instances, which we refer to as a mechanical loss. Saving a life and providing first aid is more important than the physical evidence.

1.5 TEST QUESTIONS:

T   F   1. Fingerprints are an example of class characteristic evidence.

T   F   2. Striation from a bullet or other tool is an example of individual characteristic evidence.

T   F   3. A tire impression is an example of class characteristics evidence.

T   F   4. Fingerprints can serve to prove the identity of someone without the presence of any other evidence.

T   F   5. Physical evidence recovered and properly collected in 1996 can be used as evidence in a trial in 1999.

T   F   6. Blood found at the scene of a crime can be conclusive evidence when linked to a criminal suspect, as blood is considered an example of individual characteristic evidence.

T   F   7. A glass that was knocked over and broken during a fight would be considered physical evidence.

T   F   8. At the scence of a crime, an identification card is found that belongs to no one present. The identification card would be considered physical evidence.

9. If a magistrate cannot establish that a public offense occurred or that the defendant committed the public offense, the magistrate _____ discharge the matter.

1.6 ANSWERS:

1.   **False**   Fingerprints are as individual a form of identification as there are, therefore, fingerprints are considered to be individual characteristic evidence.

2.   **True**   Striation evidence can be compared microscopically to identify specific markings to the exclusion of all others, therefore making it a form of individual characteristic evidence.

3.   This answer can be **True or False**, depending on the amount of information recorded. If the only information obtained is that of tire size and tread, then the evidence would be considered class characteristic evidence. If, however, specific information like wear of the tire tread is present and can be compared and demonstrated, that same evidence can be considered individual characteristic evidence.

4.   **True**   Unlike other forms of evidence that might need corroboration, fingerprints can stand alone as evidence in establishing identity.

5.   **True**   Physical evidence, when gathered properly, "cannot lie, forget, or be mistaken."

6.   **True**   With the advent of deoxyribonucleic acid (DNA) analysis, blood evidence is considered to be individual characteristic. Although the analysis is not 100%, the high percentages, such as one in 999,995 persons or one in 500,000, is most often high enough for the trier of fact to accept the evidence as being conclusive.

7/8.**True**   Remember, **anything that has been used, left, removed, altered, or contaminated by the victim or suspect(s) during the commission of the crime** is considered to be physical evidence.

9.   **Shall**   The magistrate has no option according to the law if it cannot be proven to the satisfaction of the magistrate that the public offense occurred.

chapter two

The first unit responder and the crime scene

With every reported crime, the unit responding to that assignment can have an impact on the outcome of the case by how and what that unit initially does during those first moments. The unit that acknowledges an assignment or "on-views" a crime must act in such a manner as to maximize the resources available. Whether the call is an in-progress, a hot run, or cold run, or responding after the fact, officers should always act with the same professional demeanor to ensure their actions will accomplish the desired goal. To maximize the resources available to officers during this critical period, the author has coined what is called implementing **"the process"**, to be utilized whenever an officer receives an assignment, whether that assignment be of a critical or less-than-critical nature. The process can also be referred to by the acronym **ARISN**. The process should become second nature to the first unit responder to any type of crime. Whether the unit is a one-person or two-person vehicle, the process can be implemented all the same.

2.1 The "process" or ARISN

What does **"the process"** consist of? It is basically five elements: (1) **A**pproach; (2) **R**ender medical aid; (3) **I**dentify additional victims or witnesses; (4) **S**ecure the scene and physical evidence; (5) Make appropriate **N**otifications. At first, the process might appear to be a long, drawn-out process. However, the five elements can be amply covered by the responding unit in a matter of minutes. Some of the elements can even be done simultaneously. Following is a brief explanation of each of these elements.

2.1.1 The approach

When approaching a crime scene, an officer must be alert to many things and not be overcome by the sometimes overwhelming nature of duties and responsibilities involved. The first decision that must be made is what mode of approach should be taken. Does the nature of the assignment require a code 3 response? Any type of driving requires the practice of defensive skills but, during a code 3 response, the officer must not only be alert for vehicle and pedestrian traffic en route, but, more importantly, must be on the lookout for other police units responding in a code 3 mode. Officers must realize that when traveling to a code 3 response, their senses are heightened and their adrenaline is circulating. Sometimes, this results in tunnel vision or failure to hear other police vehicles approaching, especially in light of the fact that sirens are directional and sometimes cannot be heard until it is too late to avoid a collision. An officer is of use to no one if he or she fails to arrive at the scene. Officers also have the responsibility of knowing the most direct route to the location assigned, enabling them to arrive expeditiously. While approaching the location, officers also must be ever vigilant, scanning the area for things or persons who look suspicious. The responding officer additonally has the responsibility of being observant of anyone who appears to be suffering from the impact of the crime. Whether that impact is of a medical or emotional nature, the officer must be aware of its existence. Should the officer size up the situation as requiring additional units for support, there should be no hesitation to radio for back-up units as quickly as possible. The old saying, "discretion is the better part of valor," is never more true than when responding to a crime. It is always better to have too much help and dismiss extra units than to not have enough units in a critical situation and wait for what appears to be an eternity for back-up. Until the officer is absolutely sure the situation is being handled appropriately, no units should be dismissed. Finally, during the approach, in their zeal to get to the scene and render assistance, officers should not overlook the presence of physical evidence. I cannot tell you how many times I have responded to a scene and found evidence altered or destroyed because it was lying in the street, and the officer who first responded to the scene ran over it with the patrol car because he or she was not "looking" for it. This may sound comical, but the consequences in some of the cases were significant. This element of the process is extremely important because of the many things the officer must be ever vigilant of during the approach. The first officer to reach the scene must establish the foundation of an investigation.

2.1.2 Rendering medical aid

When responding to the scene of a reported crime, the most important issue is to save human life or prevent additional injury. For this reason, it is imperative for first unit responders to give particular attention to anyone they come upon as they arrive on a scene that requires medical assistance. If, while officers are providing medical assistance, the scene or physical evidence becomes contaminated, altered, or lost, that is a price that must be paid. On the other hand, officers should be realistic about whether medical assistance outweighs possible evidence destruction or contamination. For example, if a victim is in medical need because of a broken bone, the officer would be ill-advised to disregard the evidence in order to attend to the broken arm. Likewise, if there is a victim with numerous superficial slash wounds, medical attention can be achieved by putting pressure bandages on the wounds until the paramedics arrive, and the officer can still maintain the integrity of the scene and the evidence. There are no hard-and-fast rules that can be applied in every situation. Regarding the medical aid issue, this is a situation where the officer needs to use a great deal of discretion. The officer should learn from those who teach first aid and life-saving measures which injuries are life-threatening and which are not, and treat the victim and the scene accordingly.

2.1.3 *Identifying additional victims/witnesses*

Upon determining that the medical issues are addressed, the officer should then begin to search the area for additional victims or witnesses. There are numerous reasons for this action. Additional victims might require additional medical assistance and the need for additional medical personnel. They can also provide needed information that will aid the officer in determining the extent of the crime, the crime scene, and any physical evidence. Additional witnesses might also serve to corroborate what actually happened and provide needed information to establish the elements of the crime, suspect descriptions, vehicle descriptions, and avenue of escape. I have personally had cases in the past where witnesses were very helpful: one in which a witness pointed out where a suspect had discarded evidence in a homicide. Upon investigating that area—the rooftop of a three-story warehouse—the homicide weapon was identified, documented, and recovered. A word of caution to the officer at this point is warranted. If there is more than one witness, the officer should make arrangements to **separate**, and keep separated, those witnesses who have something to say about what they saw. The reason for this is that everyone is subject to human frailties such as not remembering everything exactly as it happened. Many times, due to the traumatic nature of the occurrence, there will be blanks in the memory of victims and/or witnesses. As a general rule, most people cannot account for every minute during which the traumatic incident was occurring. Keeping the witnesses separated will assure that the information will be recounted in their words, not the words of witnesses with whom they have collaborated to fill in the blanks. In other words, the witnesses will tell the officers what happened, but each one will say it differently. Another word of caution is called for at this point. The officer should be suspect of statements that sound exactly alike but are given by different witnesses. A red flag should immediately be raised and the statements by witnesses and victims should be further explored. There is always the possibility that the witnesses could have collaborated before the officer's arrival, in which case the officer should take all possible steps to ascertain if that was, in fact, what happened. After obtaining all of the facts from any additional victims and/or witnesses, the officer now has the knowledge to implement the next step in the process.

2.1.4 *Secure the scene and/or any physical evidence*

Any crime will have a crime scene and some type of physical evidence associated with that crime. It is up to the officer(s) responding to the assignment to determine what that scene or evidence might be. Once the officer has made that determination, the officer and any additional units, if required, are to establish a perimeter around and protect the scene and evidence. This can be accomplished as easily as closing a door, should the scene be indoors, or placing yellow police line tape around the scene, to the more extensive use of barriers in the form of vehicles, portable "A" frames, or using police personnel as barriers, should the extent of the scene necessitate. (Figure 2.1) One must continually question **how extensive is(are) the crime scene(s)?** Officers must constantly remind themselves not to limit the scope of their investigation to determine the extent of the crime scene or where there might be the presence of physical evidence. Just as in the approach to a scene, at this point, some officers might be seeing with tunnel vision which could compromise the investigation. For example, a robbery suspect who might have sustained an injury during the commission of the crime and is bleeding, may leave a trail of blood that indicates the avenue of escape. The officer should follow that trail of blood until it disappears, and then search the immediate area for additional evidence such as money, property, weapons, possible evidence of a vehicle, or anything else that might be significant. The entire area would then be considered a secondary crime scene. If nothing else, there may be a great deal of physical evidence present. The officer must consider the area to be cordoned off and take the appropriate action. Sometimes, cordoning off a large area can be accomplished with minimal personnel. However, if there is a large crowd gathering, more personnel will be required to protect the scene and evidence. Whether the scene be indoors or outdoors, the officer must be able to account for personnel coming into and leaving the scene. This can be accomplished through the use of a **crime scene log**.

A crime scene log **is a document established by the officer to document who has entered the scene, the time in and time out, and the reason for entry into the crime scene**. A crime scene log should be maintained at all major crime scenes, and at scenes where the officer feels it is necessary, for purposes of isolation, to document the investigation. Maintaining the integrity of the scene also means keeping out other unauthorized police or emergency personnel. If they are not part of the investigation, they should not be allowed to enter the inner perimeter. That is the obvious purpose of the crime scene log: to lessen the possibility of unauthorized personnel entering into and contaminating the crime scene, (see Figure 2.2). At this point, the officer should undertake the fifth and final step in the process.

Fig. 2.1 - The figure shows how extensive a crime scene can be, especially outside the actual area of the commission of the crime. The officers, their vehicles, and yellow warning tape serve as the barriers to secure the scene and evidence located within the perimeter of the scene.

CRIME SCENE LOG				
INCIDENT REPORT NUMBER :				
TYPE OF INCIDENT:				
LOCATION:		DATE/TIME OF INCIDENT:		
OFFICER MAINTAINING LOG:		STAR:	DATE/TIME LOG STARTED:	
RELIEF OFFICER:		STAR:	DATE/TIME:	
TIME IN NAME	POSITION/TITLE	REASON FOR ENTRY		TIME OUT

Fig. 2.2 - An example of a Crime Scene Log that allows for maintaining the integrity of the scene and documenting who came into the scene and their purpose.

2.1.5 *Make notifications*

Upon identifying and determining the extent of the scene as well as the evidence, the officer is obligated to keep in mind department guidelines when making notifications. This fifth step reminds all officers that they must notify supervisors, as well as investigators or detectives who will be handling the case, and those people who will be ultimately responsible for document-ing the scene and collecting the evidence (e.g., the photo lab and/or crime scene units). In some of the smaller agencies, this may mean notification of county or state agencies to assist in the investigation. At this point in the investigation, depending on department policy and the critical nature of the crime, the first unit responder could be responsible for conducting the entire search. In any event, whatever action the officer(s) undertake, the ultimate goal of the first unit responder will be to identify, preserve, and, in some instances, collect the physical evidence. When this task is done properly, the successful investigation and conclusion of the case can be achieved.

2.2 *Nature of the scene*

The critical or non-critical nature of the crime and the scene will necessitate how specific the first unit responder must be in implementing **"the process."** Generally speaking, the more serious the crime, the greater the need there is for the specialized units to document the scene and prevent the loss of any pertinent evidence. In order to draw a distinction between the critical and non-critical nature of crime scenes, although some people would say all crime is critical, the two type are distinguishable. Simply stated, crimes and crime scenes can be categorized into **(1) major scenes** and **(2) non-major (or discretionary) scenes.**

2.2.1 *Major scenes*

These would be cases in which there is death, great bodily injury, or potential for a major investigation. Examples of this type include: **homicides; dui-cides; officer-involved shootings; felonious assaults in which death or permanent disability might occur;** or **cases where there is potential for a major investigation.**

In all major scenes, the first unit responder's responsibility rests with rendering medical aid, identification of additional victims/witnesses, identification and containment of the scene and evidence, and notifications. As a general rule, absent exigent circumstances, physical evidence **must not** be disturbed at a major crime scene prior to the arrival of the medical examiner, crime scene units, homicide investigator(s), or detectives who will be investigating the case. *A good rule of thumb for the first unit responder is to treat all major scenes as homicide scenes.* Most, if not all, of the evidence will be collected by the specialized units involved in the investigation, and first unit responders will be limited generally in their participation in the case, with the exception of what has been previously stated. Most often, the responsibility of the first unit responder will be limited to making the initial report and documenting who was present at the scene and what those units did while at the scene. At the major scene, the first unit responder has very little discretion concerning how the case will be handled.

2.2.2 *Non-major/discretionary scenes*

These scenes include all other types of crimes not categorized as major scenes. Examples would include such crimes as thefts, burglaries, and simple assaults. These types of crimes are ones in which first unit responders will use their discretion in deciding how the scene will be processed and how the physical evidence will be collected and booked. In some instances, non-major crime scenes do not require the response of investigators or detectives. The entire scene and evidence can be handled by the patrol division, depending on department policy. In non-major scenes, if the investigations units will not be responding to the scene, the responsibility of the scene and evidence rests with the most senior officer on the scene. Should there be any question about how to process the scene or evidence, the officer in charge should not be afraid to contact and consult with supervisory or investigative personnel. Remember, it is always better to err on the side of too much than not enough. This adage applies to information as well as evidence. **Do not be afraid to ask for help if you are unsure about policy, procedure, or protocol.** Mistakes are made when the senior officers are unwilling to admit that they do not have the answers and refuse to confer with others. If there is a question about whether a crime should be treated as a major or non-major scene, it is probably best to treat it as a major scene until told to do otherwise by a more senior officer or investigator. Remember, the ultimate goal is to process the scene and identify and collect the evidence in a professional manner, so that a criminal case can be established and proven, **or** to exonerate the innocent.

At any major scene, there will usually be enough officers present to permit a division of labor to accomplish the needed tasks simultaneously. The first unit on the scene will be responsible for delegating assignments until relieved by a superior officer or supervisor. Whether the scene is major or non-major, there will be three settings in which the crime takes place: **indoors, outdoors, or a combination of the two.**

2.2.3 Major indoor scenes

In addition to what was previously mentioned, there are specific things that should be done. When first entering the scene, make immediate note of the following.

1. Time
2. Entrances and exits
   a. Doors (open, closed, locked, type of lock, deadbolt, if door had to be forced for entry)
   b. Windows (opened, closed, locked, unlocked) for any signs of forced entry
3. Lights (on or off)
4. Odors (cigars, cigarettes, perfume, alcohol, gas, gun powder, unusual odors)
5. Names of persons at the scene, including emergency personnel
6. Condition of the scene (in disarray, good order, furniture tossed about, stains, position of weapons, etc.)

In addition to noting the appearance of the scene, observe the following precautions:

1. Do not touch inside door knobs, doors, or door frames
2. Do not move anything
3. Do not smoke, or use the telephone, toilet, sink, or ashtrays
4. Beware of where you step and what you touch; a good rule of thumb is to hold your hands behind your back while examining the crime scene.

2.2.4 Outdoor scenes

In addition to what has been previously mentioned, additional precautions applicable to outdoor crime scenes are as follows.

1. Establish and protect a large perimeter, especially at parks and beaches or open areas. (Remember, do not confine the bounds of your search. Do not limit yourself when searching for evidence, or searching a secondary crime scene.)
2. If foot/tire print or other impression evidence is discovered, warn all officers present to protect those areas.
3. Try to determine the suspect's route of approach and escape, and investigate the possibility of additional evidence, (e.g., discarded clothing, weapons, blood, etc.). Ifevidence is located at some distance from the main scene, the evidence should be protected as a secondary crime scene.

2.2.5 Death cases

There are four methods by which death may occur: homicide, suicide, accident, or natural causes. At any major scene, the investigating officers, detectives, or medical examiner in death cases, will make determinations regarding the case. In addition to these actions, the first unit at such scenes should also make their own observations and take note of such things as:

1. The believability of witnesses (Do they appear jittery, nervous, or anxious to leave the scene? Does their version of the incident appear questionable?)
2. Condition of the scene (as mentioned previously)
3. History of the victim and/or suspect, if known
4. Preservation of any notes found for later analysis.(fingerprints/indented writing)
5. Preservation of any medication found at the scene and the container holding the medication.

All death cases shall be treated as homicide cases until the medical examiner, or his or her deputies declare otherwise. Strange as it may sound, sometimes cases that appear to be homicides are, in actuality, suicides. As an example, I investigated a case in which the victim had five knives (none fewer than 6 inches long) stuck in his throat. The scene was extremely bloody and in total disarray. When the investigation was completed, the case was discovered to be a suicide. So keep in mind that a final determination of the type of case can be a while in coming, but without all of the necessary evidence, a successful conclusion might not ever be reached.

With every crime, there will be some sort of crime scene, however scant that scene may be. There will also be physical evidence present to identify and gather. Whether a major or non-major scene, first unit responders have the duty and obligation to perform their tasks as professionally as possible and to avoid overlooking any evidence. This includes practicing the best methods of preventing contamination. Should first unit responders be unsure of how to proceed, they should not hesitate to call for assistance. Oftentimes, officers are reluctant to ask for assistance. What is of prime inportance is not which individual can do the best job, but rather, how all can proceed collectively in a methodical manner to best identify, secure, document the scene, and, in some instances, collect the physical evidence. Often, secondary scenes are overlooked because of assumptions. Making assumptions without foundation at scenes can sometimes be costly. Officers should refrain from assuming anything until they have all the facts in their possession. Then—and only then—can the case proceed with proper investigatory vigor and circumspection.

In this chapter, the proper response to and the types of crime scenes the first unit responder might encounter were examined. Further, this chapter elaborates on some of the more frequently overlooked issues that need to be ever present in the mind of officers once they reach the crime scene. The officers must be ever mindful that crime scenes are not always going to be the same. The procedure for handling the scenes can remain constant, but the officers must be realistic enough to realize that they must be flexible and attentive to pick up the most minute differences at all crime scenes.

2.3 Review

When responding to a reported crime, every first unit responder needs to consider the following.
- **The process:** (1) the approach; (2) rendering medical aid; (3) locate and separate any additional victims/witnesses; (4) secure the scene; and (5) notifications. While at the scene, to maintain the integrity of the scene and investigation, establish a
- **Crime scene log:** A document utilized to maintain the integrity of the scene by noting who has entered the scene, the time in and out, their purpose, and their unit identifier.

Scenes will be classified according to the critical nature of the crime. The classifications are: major scenes and non-major or discretionary scenes.

- **Major crime scenes:** Death, great bodily injury, or a case that has a potential for a major investigation.
- **Non-major/discretionary crime scenes:** All other types of scenes. The responsibility of the scene and the investigation rests with the first unit arriving until such time that it is relieved by a more senior officer or a supervisor.

Death cases can be of four types: **homicide, suicide, accident**, or **natural causes**. The only person qualified to make that determination is the medical examiner or his or her deputies. All death cases shall be treated as homicides until instructed otherwise by the medical examiner or his or her representative.

The key to any successful investigation is **documentation**. If first unit responders are unclear about a policy, they should not hesitate to ask for assistance.

The ultimate purpose for an investigation is twofold:
- To find the guilty party
    AND
- To exonerate the innocent.

2.3 Test questions

T   F   1. It is not necessary to separate witnesses, as they know what happened and can relate their version in a clear and concise manner.

T   F   2. During the approach phase when responding to a crime, the officer need only concern him/herself about citizens not being aware of their presence, especially in a code 3 mode.

T   F   3. Taking the most direct route to a crime is advisable because there will probably be little, if any, physical evidence in that area.

T   F   4. Upon arrival to a scene, should an officer see a gun used in a homicide and see a victim in need of medical assistance, the officer should collect the gun first and then render medical assistance.

T   F   5. Loss or contamination of the physical evidence at a crime scene is never acceptable.

T   F   6. If a tire impression is found some distance away from the scene of a crime, the officer should document that fact, and then focus his/her attention to the immediate scene without telling others.

T   F   7. Secondary crime scenes are usually of little value as there is usually very little evidence to substantiate the crime.

T   F   8. First unit responders should always make assumptions when entering into a homicide scene, as the appearance of the scene will confirm their conclusions.

T   F   9. The only time officers must make a notification is when they feel the need to confer with the experts to confirm their suspicions.

T   F   10. Paramedics and other emergency personnel need not be directed how to enter a crime scene, as they are trained and possess the knowledge of how to skillfully approach a scene.

T   F   11. A crime scene log should only be maintained at major scenes such as homicides, suicides, or other violent crimes.

2.5 *Test answers*

1.   **False**   Witnesses *must* be separated to prevent any collaboration to "fill in the blanks."

2.   **False**   The citizen is usually not the problem, especially in a code 3 mode. If the crime is serious enough to warrant a code 3 response, other units will probably be responding to assist; and, many times, unless the other units are extremely careful, they will pose a greater hazard to police.

3.   **False**   Anytime one is approaching a crime scene, the most direct route is desirable. However, one cannot forget there may be a secondary crime scene containing evidence on that route.

4/5. **False**   The first priority at any crime scene is to render medical assistance. If that means risking losing the physical evidence, that is an acceptable loss—although not a desirable one.

6/7. **False**   Should an officer discover physical evidence some distance away from the initial scene, where that evidence is located should be considered a secondary scene and provisions should be made to safeguard any evidence discovered there until such time as the scene can be properly documented and evidence collected.

8.   **False**   The officer should *never* make assumptions at crime scenes, especially at homicide scenes. Remember, it will be the medical examiner who determines the cause of death.

9. **False** At all major scenes, officers will make proper notifications to detectives, crime scene personnel, and supervisors. At discretionary scenes, officers have this option; but as a general rule of thumb, conferring with a more experienced officer is advisable. Remember, at Non-Major Scenes, the responsibility rests with the senior officer at the scene.

10. **False** As strange as it may sound, with the exception of police personnel, many other emergency personnel are not taught how to approach crime scenes. Therefore, it is of critical importance that the officer at the scene direct all emergency personnel to the safe avenues of approach.

11. **False** A crime scene log can be used any time the officer feels it is necessary for purposes of isolation of the scene, regardless of the type of crime.

chapter three

Identifying and documenting the evidence

This chapter discusses the specific types of evidence that will enable first unit responders to be more specific in their description of evidence. Why is this important?

Eventually the officers will be required to testify about the evidence, the crime scene, and about various other factors regarding the case (see Chapter 6, "Courtroom testimony"). Officers should not have to go to court unarmed with the needed information to give proper testimony regarding the evidence. The better officers have prepared, the better the testimony will be, enabling them to give good, credible testimony in the eyes of the trier of fact.

3.1 Categories of evidence

Evidence can be categorized by its composition or type, and further subdivided into specific types. All evidence will belong to one of four general categories. The following is evidence listed by category and the more commonly observed examples:

3.1.1 Biological/Physiological

Evidence such as blood, semen, saliva, tissues, or other body fluids. This category of evidence is most commonly associated with the body of either the perpetrator or the victim.

3.1.2 Chemical

Evidence such as narcotics, chemicals commonly found in clandestine labs, legally prescribed drugs, minerals, papers, and powders associated with firearms.

3.1.3 *Physical*

Evidence such as fingerprints, footprints, impressions, toolmarks, tiremarks, restoration of serial numbers, and firearms evidence such as barrel striation, ejector, extractor, and magazine signature.

3.1.4 *Non specific/miscellaneous*

Items such as photography, dye marks, voice analysis, and the polygraph.

3.2 *Types of Evidence*

Evidence will not always fit strictly into one category. Evidence might be one of, or a combination of, the four categories. To further subdivide evidence, six types can be used: (1) trace, (2) transfer, (3) indented, (4) striated, (5) geometric, and (6) chemical.

3.2.2 *Trace evidence*

This type of evidence allows one to, as the name implies, *trace* the evidence to a certain person, place, or thing. Often, this type of evidence will be of the individual class characteristic, making it an extremely valuable type of evidence. Examples of this type of evidence are fingerprints, hairs, fibers, body fluids, clothing, paint, bullets, and glass, to name a few. Another example might be catching a suspect in possession of a victim's identification. All of the examples cited can in some way trace the evidence back to the crime, the scene, or the victim. Quite often, trace and the next type of evidence (transfer) are found to be one and the same.

3.2.2 *Transfer evidence*

Any evidence transferred from the suspect to the victim, the suspect to the scene, the victim to the suspect, or the victim to the scene. Transfer evidence is quite common in crimes of violence where a struggle has taken place and evidence was left behind. An example of linking the suspect to the victim might be skin scrapings under the fingernails of a rape victim who was fighting the suspect at the time of the crime. Bite-mark evidence is another type of evidence, in this as well as in the trace type. An example of transfer evidence linking the suspect to the scene might be a piece of clothing dropped at the scene that can be conclusively linked to the suspect. Or, a comical example that I have experienced more than once: the suspect leaves his parole identification card at the scene of a burglary, or a baseball cap with his name printed on the inside brim of the cap. An example of the victim being linked to the scene might be hairs, glasses, a contact lens, or other property of the victim are recovered where the victim said the crime occurred. One example that everyone can relate to is where blood is found at the scene of a crime or on the suspect's clothing and that blood, upon being analyzed, is determined to be the victim's blood. Strong evidence? You be the judge.

3.2.3 Indented or impression evidence

An object that has made an indentation or impression on another surface. Examples of this type of evidence would be tire or footwear impressions in mud or dirt; impressions left in snow; and/or fingerprints in paint or a clay-like substance. This type of evidence is usually readily visible and usually very obvious. In most instances, this type of evidence is very fragile and must be given the appropriate attention to not compromise, alter, or destroy the evidence (Figure 3.1).

Figure 3.1 Examples of indented/impression evidence as often seen at burglary scenes where forced entry used.

3.2.4 Striated evidence

Marks left on objects scraping together, where one object is harder than the other. Typical examples of this type of evidence would be the pry tool against a metal or aluminum window frame or striker plate of a door. A recovered bullet would also be an example of striated evidence, as the striation caused by the barrel of the gun will create a uniqueness on the surface of the bullet to the point that the evidence will be individual class characteristic and can be identified to the exclusion of all others (Figure 3.2).

3.2.5 Geometric evidence

Pieces of evidence that have assumed different shapes and sizes. Typically, this type of evidence would be associated with a broken window, or with a hit-and-run accident where the lights of the vehicle have been damaged. Geometric evidence can also allow the first unit responder to read which fracture might have occurred first, lending corroboration to a statement of a victim or witness.

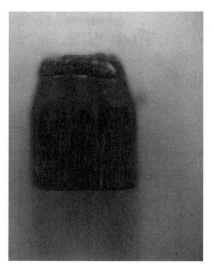

Figure 3.2 One of the most common forms of striated evidence the patrol officer will encounter is bullet evidence.

3.2.6 Chemical evidence

Narcotics, flammables, alcohol, and chemicals associated with clandestine labs and hazardous material incidents. This type of evidence is arguably the most dangerous to the first unit responder. In some instances the officer will not see or smell the evidence until it is too late and the officer has been injured. In some instances, in clandestine labs, booby traps are set with chemicals. Officers must be extremely careful when entering crime scenes where suspected chemical evidence is present. Another reason for great care is that some chemicals are light-sensitive or heat-sensitive and any change in conditions could trigger the chemicals to react, causing explosions. If the scene contains suspected chemical evidence, unless the substance is known (i.e., gasoline), the officer should back away from the scene, stay upwind, and secure the area, setting up a perimeter and making the proper notifications. Be sure to include a proper **avenue of approach** for the safety of other emergency personnel.

3.3 Use of physical evidence

Now that the officer is familiar with the *what* of physical evidence as it relates to the crime scene and its importance, knowing the *why* of physical evidence is just as important. In addition to what was discussed in Chapter One about physical evidence, what other uses does physical evidence have? **Physical evidence can:**
1. Prove a crime was committed
2. Incriminate or exonerate a suspect
3. Reconstruct a series of events

3.4 Protocol

In order to use the physical evidence to its full capacity, protocol must be established to allow for the evidence to be admissible and usable. This protocol or policy consists of establishing what is called the **chain of custody** and the proper care and collection of the physical evidence. First look at the chain of custody. Simply stated: **The chain of custody means being able to account for the evidence from the time it comes into police custody until the time it is booked and subsequently introduced as evidence in court.** Routinely, this will be accomplished by keeping a log of the evidence. On that log should be documented who handled the evidence, the date and time of the handling, and when the property was returned (Figure 3.3). **In conjunction with maintaining the chain of custody, in order for evidence to be admitted in the case, it must be relevant and not overpowering for the sake of playing on the emotions of a judge or jury.** An example of overpowering would be large glossy color photos of the stab wounds in an assault case. Additionally, for evidence to be admissible, it must be demonstrated that it is free of contamination. An example of this might be in a burglary

Incident/Report #	EVIDENCE INVENTORY		
ITEM	LOCATION FOUND	COLLECTED BY	DATE BOOKED

CHAIN OF CUSTODY

ITEM #	DESCRIPTION	RELEASED BY	RECEIVED BY	DATE	TIME

Figure 3.3 - Example of a combination form of inventory and chain of custody.

case: an officer who has taken a suspect into custody should not return the suspect to the scene of the crime because there could later be allegations that the scene was contaminated by the suspect during the second visit and not during the initial crime. This is especially true in fingerprint cases. Neither should a criminal suspect be taken back to a scene for witness identification. This could be construed as prejudicing the witnesses. To further maintain the integrity of the evidence, it must be demonstrated that the evidence was properly documented, collected, and booked. Briefly stated, the location of all evidence should be documented prior to collection. How and when this is done will depend on department policy. Some agencies do not want patrol officers photographing or sketching scenes because the officers do not possess the expertise. Other agencies want all of their initial or first unit responders to submit a small sketch of the scene and overall photos. Unfortunately, first unit responders often have Polaroid cameras, which are not known for their top-quality documentation of the scene. The best policy I can set forth is simple: all major scenes should be documented and processed by experienced crime-scene personnel, using the proper equipment to ensure that the task is properly completed. In non-major scenes, there is much more leeway available.

3.5 Documenting the evidence.

Major scene documentation is the responsibility of the experienced crime scene unit working in conjunction with the detective investigating the case. Realistically, however, proper investigative techniques sometimes must give way to the directives of higher ranking authority, especially in high-profile cases.

Having alluded to and discussed the requirement for proper documentation of a crime scene, it is also necessary to discuss how this can be achieved and under what circumstances the first unit responder should document the scene and evidence. As noted before, a major scene needs to be processed by the crime scene investigators, forensic identification personnel, the crime lab, or whatever other label has been placed on those whose training, knowledge and experience qualify them to deal with evidence of all types and scenes of all types. Simple training is no substitute for knowledge and experience. Major scenes should be processed by those who possess the knowledge, experience, and training to properly deal with the evidence. However, nothing should prevent the first unit responder from making notes of the scene and evidence, and conferring with the investigators later about the case. Keeping this in mind, the types of scenes referred to will be non-major or discretionary scenes, starting with how to document the scene and following up by stating how to collect and preserve the physical evidence.

3.5.1 Photography

The first method of documenting any scene is through the use of *photography*. The choice of equipment to be used is as varied as the types of scenes officers will encounter. Suffice it to say, as long as the camera is of good quality (a 35mm or 120 format), the scene and evidence can be adequately documented. If the only type of camera available is of the Polaroid type, then that is what the officer is stuck with using. "Something is better than nothing," as the saying goes. The purpose of photography is to document the scene as it appeared when the first officer arrived. To properly document the scene, a series of photographs must be taken. To begin, general overall shots should to be taken. These are photos in which the officer moves away some distance from the core of the scene and documents everything in the scene. The photos should be taken from a minimum of four different angles. This allows the photos to capture everything that is present at the scene and show the relationship of all the evidence at the scene. Another very important issue in documenting the scene, is the inclusion of avenues of approach and exit. This can give a perspective of what the suspect observed, as well as document possible areas of abandonment of evidence by the suspect during escape. The officers can then begin to move in closer, taking photos along the way until they get to the item(s) of main focus—the instruments of the crime. There are no hard-and-fast rules that can be practiced at every scene for photos. Each scene has its own unique characteristics. However, to properly document the scene and evidence, the information in the photos should overlap somewhat, for it is always more desirable to get too much information than not to get enough. Examples of this might be a gun, pipe, rope, tape, or any other item that might have been used to perpetrate the crime. Blood cast off or bloody impressions would be another example. (Remember, the photos should not be overly graphic simply for the sake of playing on the emotions of later observers.) As the officer closes in on the specific item, the photos might require the use of a measuring device to document size and distance. A steel measuring tape, or some type of ruler, is called for to allow the photo to demonstrate the specific area in reference to the overall scene. Another reason for the measuring device or scale in the photo is to show the actual size of the evidence and to make the task of enlargement much easier (Figure 3.4). For example, with fingerprints, a scale is needed to enable a 1:1 enlargement to be made. This might not sound so important, but there is no question that when the officer is testifying in court some months or years later on the case, the documented evidence of the case becomes all-important. When close-up photos are taken, the best method of documentation is to take a photo of the evidence with and without a scale in the photo. This alleviates or lessens the likelihood of allegations of not properly documenting the evidence, tampering with, or contaminating the evidence.

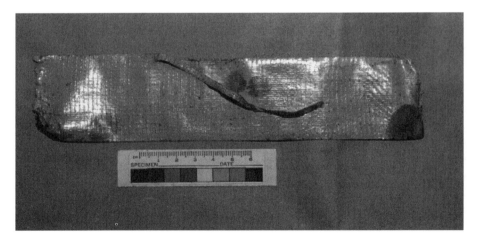

Figure 3.4   An example of fingerprints developed on tape and photographed with scale for enlargement purposes.

3.5.2 Sketching

The second method by which the scene can be documented is through the use of a *sketch*. The purpose of the sketch is to enhance or complement the photos, document the important things (evidence) in the scene, and omit extraneous (not applicable) information. Documentation can be done in one of two ways: by paces, or by measurement (preferred). To document the items in the scene, different methods can be utilized. Triangulation, right angles, or—should the scene be out in the open—surveying to establish a point of origin in which the measuring begins or is referenced to. The most widely used types of sketches are bird's-eye or overview, and cross-section (Figure 3.5). Other sketches include a perspective drawing, elevation drawing, and cross-projection or exploded view (Figure 3.6). When the measuring and documenting are complete, the sketch can be completed. Regardless of which method is chosen by the unit documenting the scene, make sure that same method is uniformly practiced throughout the process. Measurements placed within the sketch might appear to clutter the sketch. Try to keep the drawing as clean as possible. It should also include a compass to allow for orientation, as well as a legend to list pieces of evidence. This alleviates confusion, both on the part of the officer and investigators who will later be reviewing all aspects of the case. Remember, the person doing the sketch will be the one called upon to testify about the sketch. Therefore, the sketch should be as easy to read and understand as possible. Keep in mind also that the sketch will be reviewed by the prosecutor and the trier of fact—the judge or, more often, the jury. If the sketch is confusing, that might weaken the case. Photographing a scene and making a sketch can, on its face, appear to be very difficult and, in some instances, next to impossible for some officers. For these officers, it is suggested that they got over their phobia and embrace the opportunity. Unless you are planning to be a desk jockey all of your career, the best avenue of approach is to begin diagramming by doing practice diagrams so that when the real scene confronts you, you will have built up the confidence to begin conducting an investigation in a professional manner.

This chapter has discussed the types of evidence an officer might encounter. It is just as important to know what type of evidence one is looking for as it is to know where to look. The type of crime and evidence certainly will dictate how an officer proceeds at the scene of a crime. Once the evidence and the scene have been properly identified, both need to be documented through the use of photos and/or sketches. The sketch does not have to look like a draftsman or architect completed it. However, the officer must be able to make sense of the sketch, and the sketch needs to be sensible to the trier of fact.

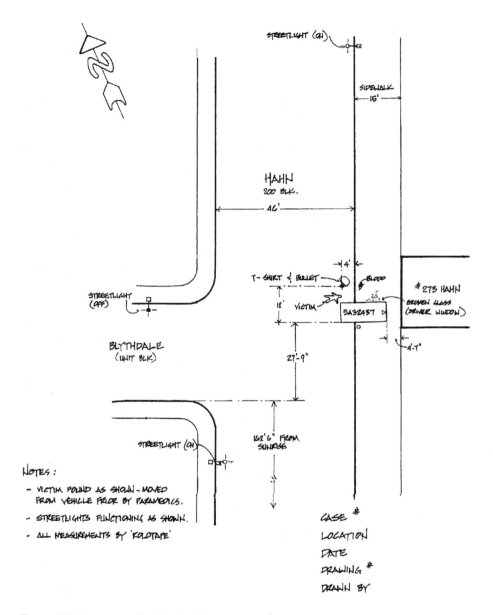

Figure 3.5 An example of a "bird's eye" sketch of an outside crime scene.

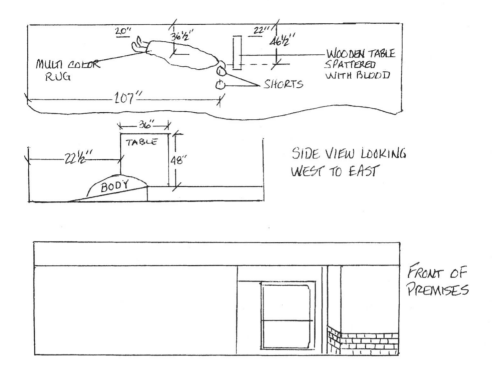

Figure 3.6 An example of a cross-projection sketch of a homicide scene.

3.6 Review

How a case will be handled depends on department policy. However, the generally accepted practices are listed and should be practiced. Evidence will be one, or a combination, of six types: (1) trace, (2) transfer, (3) indented, (4) striated, (5)gGeometric and /or (6) chemical.

Physical evidence can be used to:
1. Prove a crime was committed
2. Incriminate or exonerate a criminal suspect
3. Reconstruct a series of events

The **chain of custody** must be established in order for evidence to be admitted. The chain of custody accounts for the evidence from the time it comes into custody until it is booked and subsequently introduced into court as evidence.

The scene and evidence must be properly documented through:
1. Photographs (documenting the scene as it appears on arrival of the first officers; close-ups with and without a scale)
2. Crime scene sketch (to enhance photos and omit extraneous information)

The rules of evidence mandate that:
1. The chain of custody be maintained
2. Evidence must be relevant and not overpowering
3. Evidence must be free from contamination

3.7 Test questions

T   F   1. The purpose of crime-scene photography is to document the scene as it was when the crime was committed.

T   F   2. All photographs at a crime scene should include a scale for reference.

T   F   3. The purpose of the crime-scene sketch is to document all items at the scene that were present at the time of the crime.

T   F   4. Since fingerprints are unique, they can only be classified as trace evidence.

T   F   5. Officer Friendly responds to a homicide scene and observes a gun on the floor of the scene. The scene has been secured and all suspects, victims, and emergency personnel have been removed from the scene. The proper course of action for Officer Friendly is to pick up the gun and keep it in custody to maintain the chain of custody.

T   F   6. Officer Friendly has retrieved a piece of evidence from a crime scene and placed it in the trunk of his car as he is returning to the station. While enroute, he gets flagged down and must exit the police vehicle to conduct an investigation. He leaves the vehicle locked and secured, conducts an investigation and returns to the vehicle 5 minutes later, unlocks the vehicle and continues on to the station. Has the chain of custody of the evidence been maintained?

T   F   7. For the photography evidence to be effective, the photos must depict, very graphically, the injuries sustained by the victim.

T   F   8. If an officer detains a criminal suspect, the suspect should be taken back to the scene for questioning **and** for purposes of witness identification.

T   F   9. The officer will always be able to detect chemical evidence through the smell and/or the appearance of the evidence.

T   F   10. Physical evidence is extremely important because police are interested only in proving the guilt of a criminal suspect.

3.8 Answers

1. **False**   It is impossible to determine what the scene looked like at the time of the crime. The purpose of the photograph is to document how the scene appeared upon arrival of the officers.

2. **False**   Not all photographs require a scale. In some instances, the scale interferes with the appearance of the evidence. High-quality, close-up photos should be taken with and without a scale so that the allegation of contamination of the evidence can be eliminated.

3. **False**   The purpose of the crime-scene sketch is to enhance the photos. Extraneous information should be left out of the sketch, as it only serves to clutter the drawing.

4. **False**   Fingerprints, as well as other evidence, may not defined as being in a single category. Another example is bullets. Bullets can be classified as trace or striated.

5. **False**   Since the danger of contamination has passed and the scene is secure, there is no real reason for the officer to move the weapon, especially at a homicide scene.

6. **True**   The chain of custody has been maintained. Although Officer Friendly left the vehicle for a short period, the vehicle was locked and the integrity of the evidence was remained intact.

7. **False**   In order for the evidence to be admissible, it must not be overpowering for purposes of shock value.

8. **False**   The officer should never take a criminal suspect back to the scene of the crime. This eliminates the possibility of allegations of prejudicing witnesses or of contamination or transfer of evidence from suspect to the scene during the second visit.

9. **False**   Chemical evidence is arguably the most dangerous type of evidence the officer will encounter because it is not always detectable.

10. **False**   The purpose of the investigation is to incriminate the guilty, but also to exonerate the innocent.

chapter four

Collecting the evidence

This chapter will begin to examine the different types or pieces of evidence an officer might encounter at a crime scene and how to properly collect and package that evidence. Remember, anything can potentially be evidence from a crime. This means that, although not specifically listed in this chapter any item is potentially eligible to become pertinent, and the officer is responsible for proper collection and packaging of each piece of evidence as the circumstances dictate. Also keep in mind that once evidence has been contaminated or lost, there is no method for decontamination or reconstruction of this evidence to its original condition. The amount of evidence is sometimes difficult to determine. However, it is important to gather all potential physical evidence before it can be lost or contaminated. Remember, it is always better to have too much than too little evidence. General guidelines necessitate that most items of evidence will be placed in a standard paper envelope, bag, or box, or, where the item is too large, a property tag should be attached to the item (Figure 4.1). When the evidence is marked, it must be marked with the collecting officer's initials and/or star number, but only when such marking will not contaminate, alter, or destroy the items of evidence.

4.1 Commonly encountered evidence and packaging

Some specific guidelines for packaging and booking of certain types of evidence are listed as follows.

4.1.1 Clothing

Clothing can generally be packaged in the standard paper envelope or bag and sealed at the seams with the officer's initials and/or star number. On the clothing item itself, the officer should place his or her particular mark or star number in an easily found location, using indelible ink that will contrast with the clothing. Surprisingly, there have been instances where officers have placed their mark on an item, only to later realize that their mark has become invisible by blending in with the material. A good rule of thumb on clothing is to try to keep the identifying mark close to the label of the item; it is much easier found in that location. On trousers, it is generally a good idea to mark the item on the waistband. The idea is to maintain a general location and consistency when marking the item. It is much easier and looks more professional in court when officers are able to quickly locate their identifying mark on the item, instead of fumbling in front of a judge or jury to locate the mark. Where the collection and packaging of clothing changes slightly is when there is the presence of additional evidence on a garment, such as body fluid, hairs, fibers, paint chip, or where a hole or rip in the clothing has been caused by a gunshot or cutting, or a struggle during the course of the crime. This is where proper handling becomes critical to prevent the loss of that additional evidence.

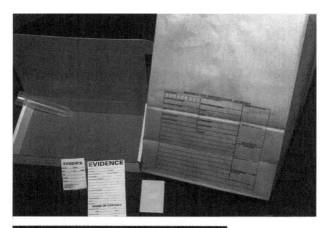

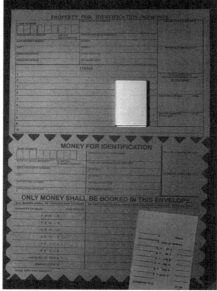

Figure 4.1   Examples of the various containers and labels used for packaging of evidence.

Before packaging the item of clothing, additional evidence must be removed and booked separately. This is quite easily accomplished by picking the piece of evidence off the clothing with the glove-covered hand or with forceps. The idea is to not lose or contaminate the additional evidence that has been located. Once removed from the clothing, hairs, fibers, paint chips, and the like should be placed into a bindle, and then placed into a larger envelope where the item will be permanently stored. When sealing the large envelope, officers should place their initials and star number on the flaps, then seal with transparent tape. Where the clothing contains body fluid, before packaging the item, it **must** be air-dried. Depending on the extent of the body fluid, it will possibly not dry before the officer leaves his/her shift, making packaging of the item inadvisable. Most agencies have a drying room where items can dry overnight and be packaged the next day or next watch. When the body fluids will be analyzed later, the packaging container should be placed in a freezer. (Recent controversy over whether items need to be frozen with the advent of DNA technology remains. Always proceed according to department policy.) The container itself should also be labeled "BIO-HAZARD" to alert anyone coming into contact with that container that there might be something inside that could be potentially harmful to them, and "Freezer" to allow for the proper preservation of the fluids. In addition, other appropriate information should be placed on the packaging container, such as the case number, the date, the location, the unit identifier, the officer's name and star number, and a brief description of the contents (Figure 4.2). Where the clothing will be folded inside the container, paper should be placed between the folds of the clothing to prevent any transfer of fluids onto another part of the clothing (Figure 4.3). Where there is a rip, tear, or hole in the clothing, the item should be carefully folded so as to not disturb that particular part of the clothing. Where the hole or tear is located, that portion of the garment should be folded flat and protected by placing paper over that portion of the clothing. Where there is apparent gunshot residue on or in the clothing, before placing the garment into the packaging container, place paper over that area containing the gunshot residue, and then place the clothing in the appropriate container and mark the container.

4.1.2 Firearms

Firearms should be handled so as to minimize contamination or destruction of any evidence, specifically fingerprints or other trace evidence. Small guns, pistols or pistol types, are to be handled by the checkered grips or by the edge of the trigger guard. To properly transport the firearm, a box and string should be utilized. Tie the string through the trigger guard so the gun is suspended and connect the ends of the string to the sides of the box. In this way, the gun will not rub against or bump into anything thereby lessening the chance of dislodging additional evidence, if there is any present.(Figure 4.4). Long guns, such as rifles or shotguns, should be handled by the butt and trigger guard of the weapon. Before booking or packaging the weapon, the officer should place his/her identifying mark, using

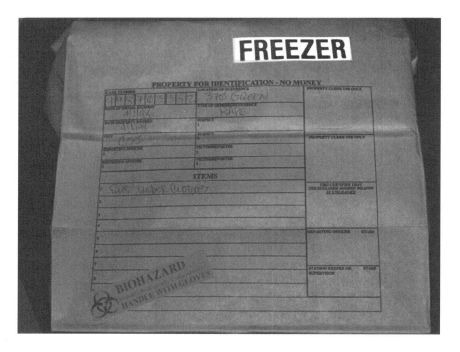

Figure 4.2 Example of basic information contained on booking containers to be used in conjunction with labeling to alert others to potential hazards contained within the package.

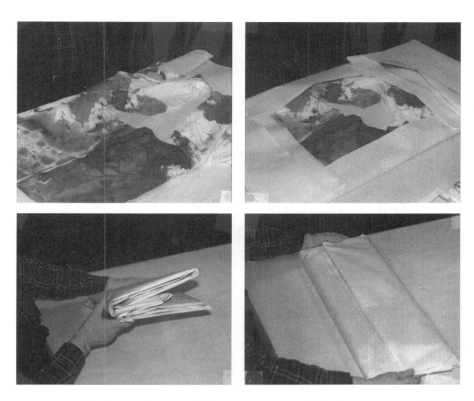

Figure 4.3   Clockwise, from top left, steps in properly booking a piece of bloody clothing by layering paper between the clothing to prevent cross-contamination or transfer of blood onto other parts of garment.

indelible ink or etching marker, into the frame of the weapon. Depending on the circumstances, the weapon should be diagrammed and a note should be made of what type of cartridges are in the gun and in what order they are located, (what chamber in the cylinder or in what position in the magazine or clip). In some instances, suspects load cartridges in a certain order, which can serve as their signature. The weapon can then be unloaded and the ammunition placed in a separate envelope, and then placed in the same container as the firearm. **Under no circumstances should a loaded firearm be booked or packaged as evidence.** The officer should also be aware that there may be trace evidence inside the barrel of the firearm in the form of hairs, blood, fiber, or skin. Should that be the case, the officer can easily obtain that evidence by using a sterile cotton swab to remove the trace evidence from the barrel. If the blood in the barrel is dry, that must be noted in the report and the appropriate notification made. The blood might be lost if it is not collected. **All firearms needing to be processed for fingerprints should not be booked, unloaded, or magazines removed.** Rifle or long-gun ammunition should be booked in a separate container and labeled as such.

Also, where the firearm is an antique or of great value, it should not be devalued during booking. If need be, use a booking tag and attach it to the firearm.

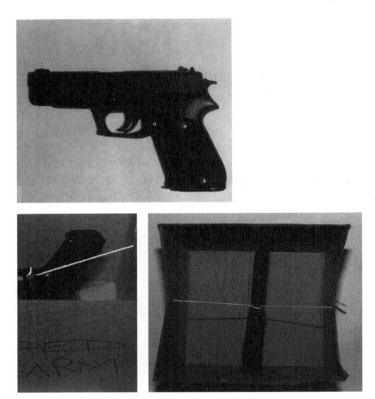

Figure 4.4 Example of the proper manner in which a firearm should be transported.

4.1.3 Bullets and Cartridge Casings

Often, when responding to the scene of a shooting or shots fired, officers might retrieve spent bullets, cartridges, or cartridge casings. Prior to moving any bullets or casings, they should document the location and include that information in the incident report. Officers may be required to document the location with the aid of a sketch. Action should be based on department policy and guidelines. The evidence can then be transported appropriately in a suitable container (preferably paper). Upon packaging the evidence (bullets or casings), officers should mark the container, not the evidence, to alleviate the possibility of destruction of minute evidence such as striation, breech face markings, ejector, extractor marks, or magazine signature. Some agencies now have the capability of categorizing, tracing, and comparing bullets based on the striation shown on the bullets. There are varying systems used for this purpose (Figure 4.5). Some agencies mandate marking the bullets and casings. Although general guidelines are set forth herein, an officer is still bound by his/her own department policy. Where the agency insists on the marking of bullets and cartridges, the proper place to mark a bullet is on the base (Figure 4.6). At any other place on the bullet, the risk of losing striated evidence is present. The proper place to mark a cartridge is in the mouth of the cartridge. Although difficult, it can be done. The difficulty occurs especially with small-caliber casings such as 22 or 25 cal. In defense of these guidelines: the less evidence is handled, the less likelihood it will be altered or contaminated.

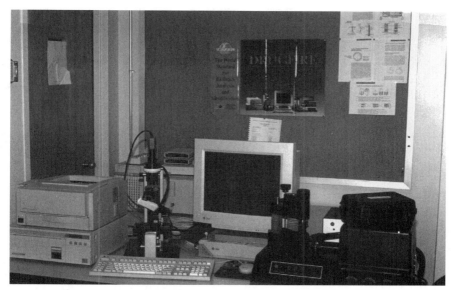

Figure 4.5 Pictured are the components of a drugfire system.

4.1.4 Gunshot Residue (GSR)

Commonly known as GSRs or SEM (scanning electron microscope) blocks, this type of evidence is very easily lost if caution is not observed. This type of evidence can determine the amount of residue on suspects or their clothing. The process consists of simply taking samples from a suspect's hands via a sticky surface tab and having the tab analyzed (Figure 4.7). In cases where GSRs are to be administered, the subject to be sampled should be handcuffed with his/her hands apart and not be allowed to use the washroom or go to the bathroom unescorted until the administration of the test. Where the individual is wearing long-sleeved clothing, that clothing should be booked for later analysis of gunshot residue. Should the officer suspect that shots were fired from a vehicle, in some instances, GSRs can be performed on the vehicle. It is best to consult with supervisors or detectives in those instances where it may be necessary to have a vehicle sampled.

Once the samples are taken, they can be packaged in a standard paper envelope and sealed appropriately with the officer's mark and transparent tape. Information that should be included with the sample in the property container at a minimum should consist of: time the sample was taken, time the shooting took place, from whom the sample was taken, who took the sample, how many shots were fired, the type of ammunition used, whether the shooting occurred indoors or outdoors, what type of occupation the suspect has, and any other pertinent information (Figure 4.8).

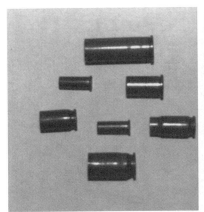

Figure 4.6 Pictured are different types of casings (top left); various bullets (top right); examples of how to package firearms evidence (bottom).

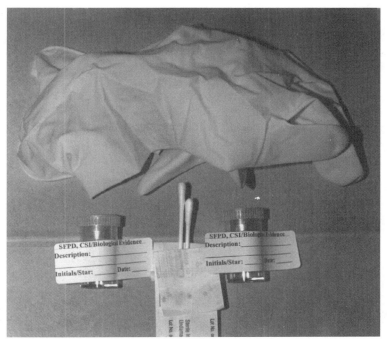

Figure 4.7 Examples of the equipment used in the taking of gunshot residue. sticky tabs, swabs, latex gloves, labels on containers, and the paper container in which to place the items.

4.1.5 Weapons (other than firearms) or other tools used in crimes (screwdrivers, hammers, lock picks, knives, sharp instruments, etc.)

Any time a weapon or tool is deemed to be evidence, appropriate care can mean the difference between placing the tool at the scene of the crime or just having something consistent with its occurrence. Before removing a weapon or tool, always document the location of the item. This can easily be done by writing a few words about the location or by making a small sketch in relation to the scene. If a suspect is in possession of a tool, note where on the suspect the tool was located. When the weapon or tool has other trace evidence on it, that trace evidence should be collected and packaged separately from the tool itself. For example, if there is blood on the blade of a knife, it is improper to simply book the knife with the blood on the blade and mark "freezer " on the container. When metal is placed in and later taken out of a freezer, it develops moisture on it called condensation. That condensation can compromise the blood on the blade. Therefore, before booking the knife, a swab of the blood on the blade should be taken and booked separately and placed in the freezer. The knife then can be packaged in the normal fashion. Where the tool or weapon has recently been broken or altered, as in the blade of a screwdriver having one of the corners broken off because it was used as a pry tool, be sure to go to great lengths to properly handle and package that item. Use bubble wrap or other appropriate wrapping to cushion the end of the tool to maintain its integrity. A mold or cast can later be taken of the tool and compared with the cast taken at the scene of the crime. Hopefully, there will be a match of the impression and the tool cast. When officers mark the tool, the best place to put their initials and/or star numbers is where the mark will be the least obtrusive or that will not alter or contaminate the tool. As the old saying goes, common sense and good judgment can go a long way in this instance. It is not difficult to appropriately book a tool or weapon.

This provides a basic overview that should be applicable in all cases where the officer will be booking weapons or tools of the crime. Should the tool be suspected of containing latent fingerprints, the item should not be marked or packaged until the latent-print person has processed the item.

GSR DATA SHEET

Subject's Name _____ Case number _____
Type of Case _____ Unit handling _____
Inspector/Detective _____ Date _____

Subject and Incident Information

[ ] Right handed   [ ] Left handed   [ ] Unknown
Occupation _____
Activity prior to shooting _____
Location of shooting [ ] indoor   [ ] outdoor   [ ] unknown
Number of shots fired _____
Date and Time of the shooting _____ _____
Date and Time sample taken _____
If subject was dead at the scene, was firearm found in his hand? _____
If Yes, which one? [ ] Right [ ] Left   If no, relative location to deceased.
_____

Firearm Information

[ ] Revolver [ ] Pistol [ ] Rifle [ ] Shotgun [ ] Other _____
Make & Model _____ Caliber _____
Barrel Length _____

Ammunition Information

Ammunition Brand _____ Caliber _____
Bullet Style [ ] Round nose [ ] Hollow point [ ] Wadcutter [ ] other_____
Bullet Type [ ] Full metal jacket [ ] Semi-jacketed [ ] Other _____

Additional information
_____
_____

Prepared by _____ Star/Badge #_____

Figure 4.8 Example of gunshot data sheet and information recorded.

4.1.6 Questioned Documents

A questioned document (QD) is basically paper evidence. Included in the definition of QD are checks, credit card receipts, threat and extortion letters, robbery notes, suicide notes, business records, and the like. Where officers encounter questioned document evidence, they should follow some simple rules, as follows.

1. Do not allow the suspect to handle the document.
2. Preserve the document for latent fingerprints and/or indented writing.
3. Do not write on or mark the document in any way.
4. Store and transport the document in an envelope. Use an envelope that is large enough to allow the questioned document to be stored in it without the need to make any folds in the document. Write the description of the evidence on the storage envelope before placing the document inside.
5. Keep a record of each document, including the date, place, and from whom it was obtained, and include that information in the report.
6. Keep documents away from excessive light, heat, and moisture.
7. Never attempt to reconstruct a torn or damaged document.

With questioned documents, the questioned-document examiner, in some instances, can develop significant information from the document through a process called ESDA (electrostatic dusting apparatus) as well as the possible presence of fingerprint evidence.

The above-listed rules are crucial when handling questioned document evidence. The best type of container, as with most other evidence, is paper (Figure 4.9).

4.1.7 Money

Money should be packaged in a separate type of envelope. Most agencies utilize money-for-identification envelopes. The money should be counted out, and the designation of dollar and coin amounts should be placed on the outside of the container, both in numbers and in longhand writing. Two envelopes should be utilized, a small envelope within a larger envelope. This makes keeping track of the money much easier, especially if there are significant amounts of money involved in the case.

4.1.8 Jewelry

This evidence should also be packaged separately from all other evidence. Discretion should be used when deciding whether to mark jewelry. Its intrinsic value should be one of the main determining factors. For example, if the jewelry is antique or of great value, one might think twice about marking it. If the jewelry is what is called "fashion" or "costume" jewelry, perhaps marking the item is not out of the question. If the item is to be marked, use indelible ink. A good rule of thumb is that the jewelry itself should not be marked, but rather the container in which the jewelry is to be placed should be marked. A standard-size paper envelope can be used. Some agencies use a special envelope for jewelry. Whichever the case, officers are cautioned to use the appropriate container when packaging jewelry. If there are numerous pieces of jewelry, some type of packaging paper to keep the items separate might be useful. Once packaged, the container can be marked appropriately with the officer's initials and star number and sealed with transparent tape.

Figure 4.9 Two views of a demand note that has been processed for the presence of latent fingerprints. The dark spots represent latent fingerprints.

4.1.9 Chemical

Most chemical evidence will be handled by those investigators properly trained and equipped. Most first unit responders will only contain and preserve scenes that have chemical evidence present. Most chemical evidence will be present during a hazardous-material spill or where a clandestine lab has been discovered. In either situation, the first unit responder is not provided with the proper training to handle such incidents. The proper authorities should be called to handle this type of incident. Where the first unit responder can play a part in chemical evidence is in the instance of a fire, whether caused naturally or by suspected arson. In the cases of suspected arson, the officers might be required to book some of the evidence that could contain a petroleum product or accelerator, such as gasoline or kerosene. For this, the officer should place the item containing the chemical into an air-tight, opaque container, and seal and mark the container appropriately. Another type of chemical evidence officers might be required to collect is following a DUI incident. Proper containers should be provided to the officers at the collection site.

4.1.10 Suspected drugs/narcotics

When an officer encounters this type of evidence, prior to handling it, for safety reasons the officer should put on latex gloves. A minimum of double-gloving is suggested, as officers with single-layer latex gloves have been reported to absorb the chemicals and to have become affected adversely after prolonged handling. Suspected drugs/narcotics should be packaged in a container that clearly states "**Analyzed Evidence.**" Most of the evidence encountered by an officer will be small packages in the form of plastic bags of marijuana, heroin, cocaine, crack, or larger containers of plastic, encased in duct tape, containing what is known as a brick or kilo (2.2 lbs.). Most of this type of evidence can be placed in a paper envelope marked "Analyzed Evidence." Where the container(s) are too large or too numerous, larger bags or boxes can be utilized. Where plants have been seized, tags can be used to tag each one. In any case, officers need to clearly mark their initials and star numbers on the smaller containers and on the tags of larger items. There should also be a central repository where the suspected drugs/narcotics can be placed for storage until the crime lab can analyze the evidence. Care and caution should be used when handling these items. Many times, the chemicals used in the processing of narcotics are very potent and can be absorbed through the skin or inhaled, as many narcotics officers will attest.

4.1.11 Miscellaneous Items

Many other items not specifically mentioned in this section can generally be booked or packaged in standard-size property envelopes. Where the items are very small (e.g., paint chips, hairs, fibers), a bindle or small envelope can be used to hold the item of evidence. Then place the small envelope into the larger, standard-size, property envelope. Marking of the item(s) should be accomplished with indelible ink or etched into the item, then placing them into the envelope and properly sealing it and marking it with all appropriate information (report number, date, unit identifier, officer's name and star number, location of the incident, type of incident, suspect(s) if known, and a description of the contents).

4.1.12 Latent fingerprints

Latent fingerprints will be the most common type of evidence the first unit responder encounters. It is also one of the most fragile types of evidence. One of the unique aspects about latent-fingerprint evidence is that in many instances it is the only way to prove a crime, and the evidence could possibly stand on its own merit. Another unique quality of fingerprints is that they can be identified as belonging to a particular individual to the exclusion of all others. There is no other type of evidence that comes close to that accomplishment, with the exception of DNA. For the first unit responders, protecting items that might contain latent fingerprints is not difficult if they know what to look for. The philosophy generally applied for the patrol officer is to look for items or surfaces that might contain prints—not for the presence of latent fingerprints themselves. In many instances, if what appears to be latent prints can be seen, they are probably not that good. Another important reason for the first unit responder to give special attention to looking for possible latent prints is that identifications can now be made with a partial latent fingerprint more easily than in the past due to the development of what is called **AFIS** (**A**utomated **F**ingerprint **I**dentification **S**ystem) (Figure 4.10). This system consists of a sophisticated electronic computer that searches a database for fingerprint patterns similar to the ones entered in by the latent-print examiners or identification technicians. When the search is complete, a list of candidates is presented to the operator. The list is then checked against the latent fingerprints lifted or developed from the scene and/or evidence. The actual identification is still performed the old-fashioned way: by the human eye, by placing the known and latent prints side by side and comparing. When the examiner is satisfied that the prints match, a conclusion is drawn based on the evidence. The ability of investigators to now make identifications based on latent fingerprints has soared with the advent of AFIS and new development techniques. Hence, the importance of the first unit responder to identify, preserve and collect evidence that might contain latent prints has never been more important.

The following is an outline of what the first unit responder should be looking for at the crime scene. As a general rule, smooth, glossy, nonporous surfaces are the best place to look for latent prints. However, officers should not limit their scope to only these types of surfaces. Latent prints can and have been developed on a variety of surfaces from paper to unfinished wood. At homicide scenes, latent prints have been developed on bodies of the deceased. The best manner in which an officer should approach the issue of fingerprint evidence is to simply look at what is out of place and what was touched by the suspect/perpetrator. Further, utilizing good interview skills, obtain from the victim or any witnesses what the suspect(s) touched during their presence at the crime. Once these particular items have been identified, secure those items and preserve them for the crime scene/crime lab or forensic-identification personnel. If items containing possible print(s) must be transported back to the station, this can easily be accomplished by placing the item in a box or paper envelope. Be very careful how the item is handled; do not assume that by putting on a pair of latex gloves that you can touch the item and not leave prints. You might destroy any prints already on that item. Try to handle items by their edges or in a place that will be least likely to damage potential latent fingerprints. Once at the station, clearly mark on the container, "DON'T TOUCH. BEING HELD FOR PRINTS," or something similar to let other personnel know not to touch. Law enforcement personnel tend to be very curious and may be tempted to examine evidence, which can compromise it. After the items have been processed for latent prints, the item can be booked in the usual fashion. The fingerprint evidence will be taken by the CS/CL/FID personnel, booked, and held in their offices.

NOTE: Some agencies want their patrol personnel to process items for prints. In those situations, the best course of action is to follow department policy regarding fingerprint processing.

Figure 4.10 An example of the hardware involved in an AFIS system. Pictured are the monitor, the reader, and keyboard for accessing information.

4.1.13 Blood

When there is blood evidence involved in a case, first unit responders should view the blood in terms of its overall importance to the crime to assist them in determining whether the blood should be merely photographed, noted, and diagrammed, or whether samples of the blood should be taken. For example, if the crime is a simple assault and the victim is the only one who suffered blood loss, possibly from a bloody nose, the importance of collecting the blood is certainly less significant than in the case of an assault with a deadly weapon where there may be blood at the scene and on the instrument of the crime. Most agencies, where there is blood to be collected, will use their crime lab or crime-scene personnel. This is because those personnel have been trained, not only in the gathering of blood, but also in how to read and document the blood at the scene, a process called **bloodstain-pattern analysis**. However, in those situations where first unit responders will be collecting the blood, the collection process is not as complicated as one might assume. Where blood is collected, it must first be documented. This can be done with a combination of photos and sketches, or simply noting where the blood was retrieved. Before collecting any blood, the officer should put on gloves to prevent contamination; but more importantly, to protect the officer from the various diseases that might be contained in body fluids.

There are two methods most commonly used to collect blood—by swab and by swatch. Both are basically the same in that they accomplish the same thing. Where the blood is wet, simply dip the tip of a swab into the blood and let it absorb until the swab is saturated. The same principle applies using a swatch of cloth. One must also submit a standard for comparison. Simply take a sample from the surface where the blood was removed, preferably as close to the blood sample as possible. Prior to booking the samples, they must be allowed to air-dry and then placed into a suitable paper container and labeled "BIOHAZARD" and "FREEZER." Where the blood is dried, depending on the amount of blood, one of two methods can be utilized. The first is similar to the one previously mentioned except that one must add a couple of drops of distilled water to the swab or swatch before trying to obtain the blood. Do not saturate the swab or swatch with water, as this will dilute the sample. Where there is much more dried blood, a bindle can be used and placed under the dried blood, and a sanitary blade can be used to scrape the blood into the bindle. The dried blood can then be packaged. Blood evidence, like fingerprints, can identify someone. However, unlike fingerprints, blood analysis is still not 100% accurate. The percentages are high enough to exclude a greater percentage of the population, but not all, as fingerprints can do.

Remember: at scenes where blood might be present as the result of a crime, look up, look down, look all around. Remember to document what you see. Bloodstain-pattern analysis can be used by those properly trained to reconstruct the sequence of events based on the appearance of the blood.

4.1.14 *Vehicles*

Where vehicles are involved in crime, the general rule of thumb is to tow the vehicle to an impound area where it can be properly processed (photos, diagrams, latent-fingerprint work). Many times, at the crime scene, the conditions are less than satisfactory (weather, lighting, etc.). However, if the possibility of losing evidence exists when the vehicle is towed, that evidence should be retrieved prior to towing the vehicle and booked by the officer. In instances where an auto has been boosted, the victim can drive the vehicle to the station or to the impound where the vehicle can be processed. Again, some departments want their patrol personnel to process vehicles for latent prints and submit those prints to latent-print examiners for identification. Officers must again proceed accordingly. It is suggested that in all major crimes where a vehicle is involved, the best course of action is to tow the vehicle and properly process it at the impound.

4.2 Review

This chapter focused the many types of evidence the first unit responder might encounter. The list is by no means all-encompassing. However, the attempt was made to present the more frequently encountered types of evidence the officer will be dealing with and how to properly package those items of evidence. From the types of evidence listed, the officer should be equipped to adapt packaging guidelines to any situation.

- At a minimum, all containers should bear the incident report number, the date of occurrence, the date of booking, the unit identifier, the officer's name and star number, the location of the occurrence, a victim, a suspect if known, and a description of the contents of the container.
- When the evidence will be analyzed later, such as blood or other body fluid, "**FREEZER**" should be written on the container. When the evidence contains or consists of some sort of body fluid, "**BIOHAZARD**" should be written on the container. These notations warn others who will be handling the containers to be very cautious.
- **Clothing** should be packaged in a standard-size paper envelope or, where there are numerous items of clothing, a bag or box of some sort. If the clothing is wet with blood, water, or other liquid, it must be air-dried before being placed into the package. If there is other trace evidence on the garment, the trace evidence should be removed and booked separately.
- **Loaded Firearms** should never be booked. Handling a firearm should be done only by the checkered grips, trigger guard, or in a place least likely to contaminate the surface if the gun is to be preserved for prints. Do not place anything into the barrel of the weapon to transport. If there is additional trace evidence in the barrel, a swab can be used to collect the evidence and book it separately from the firearm. Marking of the firearm should be done by marking on the frame of the weapon with indelible ink or etching. Do not destroy the value of the firearm when marking it.
- **Bullets and cartridge casings** can easily be packaged. When packaging the bullets and cartridge casings, the best method is to mark the

container. However, some agencies insist on marking the evidence. If this is the case, bullets should be marked at the base, and cartridges should be marked inside the mouth. Valuable striation evidence can be obtained from bullets and cartridge casings.

- Where **GSR samples** will be taken from criminal suspects, do not tell suspects they will be sampled. Handcuff the hands apart, and do not let suspects wash their hands or use the restroom unescorted prior to the administration of the GSR. Should the suspect be wearing a long-sleeved garment, do not be afraid to book the garment to be later analyzed for the presence of gunshot residue.
- **Questioned documents** can yield a great deal of information when properly obtained and booked. Keep in mind that fingerprints can be developed from paper, so when touching QD, do so by the edges. Properly package the evidence as the document can also be tested for indented writing, and do not try to reconnect torn pieces of the document by taping them together. Comparisons can be done by the crime lab to match the pieces of the document. Never write on the container when the QD is inside the envelope or container.
- **Money** should always be packaged in a separate container specifically designated for money. Money should not be marked; rather, the container or the money envelope should be marked. Both a small and large envelope should be utilized, one inside the other. On the envelope, the amount should be written in numbers as well as longhand.
- **Jewelry** should be packaged in separate containers from other evidence. Use good judgment in marking jewelry. Marking the container is the preferable course of action; this relieves the officer of devaluing the piece of evidence should it be fine jewelry.
- **Suspected drugs/Narcotics** should be packaged in an analyzed-evidence envelope. For safety reasons, officers booking drugs should wear gloves (doubled), as some drugs can be absorbed topically.
- **Chemical evidence** is arguably the most dangerous type of evidence. Officers should be most cautious when dealing with possible chemical evidence. Stay up-wind and do not drastically change the conditions under which the chemicals are present (light, heat, mixing chemicals, etc.). To book the evidence, an opaque, air-tight container should be utilized.
- **Latent fingerprints** have the potential of being anywhere. Proper care and caution need to be exercised when looking for items that might contain latent fingerprints. Smooth, glossy, nonporous surfaces are best, but fingerprints can potentially be developed on almost any surface, including bodies. Unique to fingerprints is their ability to identify someone to the exclusion of all others—100% accuracy.
- **Vehicles** can be processed at the scene, but the best course of action is to tow the vehicle to an impound area where the task of processing the vehicle can be done properly under ideal conditions. If the possibility

exists that evidence might be lost during the towing of the vehicle, that evidence should be retrieved and booked prior to the tow.

4.3 Test questions

T   F   1. If evidence has been contaminated or altered, it can be restored to its original condition.

T   F   2. Before booking any item that contains body fluids, it is always advisable to air the item.

T   F   3. Where an item cannot be air dried before the conclusion of the watch, booking the item is permissible.

T   F   4. The best method to pick up a firearm and transport it is by placing an object, preferably a pencil or other small object, down the barrel.

T   F   5. Booking a pistol/revolver and the cartridges in the same container is permissible.

T   F   6. Booking a loaded firearm is permissible as long as the package is labeled properly.

T   F   7. Since the likelihood of developing fingerprints on a rifle or shotgun is relatively slim, it is permissible to transport a rifle or shotgun by picking it up by the stock, butt, or barrel.

T   F   8. The best place to mark a bullet is on the tip or side of the bullet.

T   F   9. Where GSR blocks will be administered, it is always best to tell the suspect while enroute to the holding area.

T   F   10. If GSR blocks are performed on a suspect, there is no need to collect long-sleeved garments.

T   F   11. When packaging questioned documents that have been torn into pieces, it is always advisable to attempt to carefully tape the pieces back together before placing the item into a booking container.

T   F   12. Once a questioned document has been processed for indented writing, no further evidence can be retrieved from the document.

T   F   13. Chemical evidence should be booked much the same as other evidence by packaging in paper and properly labeling with the officer's initials and star number.

T   F   14. Since latent fingerprints are so fragile, the only surfaces that will contain prints are smooth, glossy, or nonporous.

T   F   15. The AFIS computer is an electronic computer that identifies criminal suspects.

4.4 Test answers

1. **FALSE** Once contaminated, altered, or destroyed, a piece of evidence cannot be reconstituted.

2. **TRUE** If an item is booked containing wet body fluid, bacteria could develop that could cause degradation of the fluid, rendering later analysis more difficult or even impossible.

3. **FALSE** See Answer #2.

4. **FALSE** The best place in which to handle a firearm is by the checker grips or by the edge of the trigger guard. Placing an object in the barrel might cause a change in the striation markings.

5. **TRUE** Booking a pistol/revolver in the same container is permissible, provided, however, that the cartridge, bullets, and/or casings are in a separate package within the container.

6. **FALSE** A loaded firearm should *never* be booked under any circumstances.

7. **FALSE** The long gun can be handled by the edge of the trigger guard or by the rubberized portion of the butt—any place unlikely to leave or remove possible fingerprint evidence.

8. **FALSE** The preferable method of packaging a bullet is by marking the container. However, if the bullet must be marked, the best place is at the base. At the side or tip might result in lost or altered striate evidence.

9. **FALSE** Never tell suspects that they will be tested for gunshot residue. This can prevent them from attempting to destroy or eliminate the evidence.

10. **FALSE** There may be additional gunshot residue on the garment.

11. **FALSE** The reconstruction of the note or other document will be done by the criminalist.

12. **FALSE** Other types of evidence can be obtained, including fingerprints, inks, and handwriting analysis.

13. **FALSE** Of all the evidence encountered by the patrol officer, chemical evidence can potentially be the most dangerous. Chemical evidence should always be packaged in an air-tight, opaque container.

14. **FALSE** There are a myriad of surfaces from which fingerprints can be developed with the advent of new technology.

15. **FALSE** The identification of a criminal suspect through fingerprints is undertaken by a latent-fingerprint examiner. Through the use of a comparator, or magnifying glass, the examiner views both the latent and known prints of the suspect, side by side, and renders an identification.

chapter five

Fingerprints and the crime

As mentioned in Chapter Four, fingerprints are the most common form of evidence the first unit responder will encounter. Because of the ubiquitous nature and the potential of fingerprint evidence in a criminal case, the necessity of having knowledge about the varied aspects of fingerprints is paramount for the first unit responder. This chapter is not designed to make experts of first unit responders, but rather to give them greater insight into fingerprints and their potential; this will allow first unit responders to better investigate and identify potential areas and items that might contain prints.

5.1 Victim interaction

The first unit responder must remember that the victim has just been traumatized by an event in which they had little or no control. The officer should want to always remember that the traumatized victim might not be in the best frame of mind, nor be as forthcoming with information as the officer would wish. To that end, the officer should always be as sympathetic as possible and direct the interview to establish the greatest probability of identifying items and surfaces that might contain latent fingerprints. Where items have been identified, the officer should instruct the victim to set those items aside for processing at a later time if the officer will not be the one processing those items. The officer should instruct the victim to handle the items by the edges to avoid contaminating or compromising any latent prints that could be present. Preferably, the officer should set aside the items.

Allow the victim to resume normal activity as soon as possible, as the victim has been inconvenienced and traumatized enough already. Where items containing possible latents can be removed from the premises, the officer should make every attempt to explain to the victim the purpose for such action and, where appropriate, issue a receipt. If an item cannot be removed, safeguards should be initiated to protect it until the surface can be processed, as in the case of a countertop or table at a robbery scene.

The uniqueness of fingerprints was discussed in Chapters One and Four. In addition, first unit responders need to become familiar with terminology and be able to express in court and to others who will be involved in the investigation, and specifically what they are talking about when referring to fingerprints. Latent fingerprints can be the most damaging form of evidence because of their uniqueness—100% to the exclusion of all other suspects. Officers should also realize that fingerprints are one of the most fragile types of evidence in a criminal case, and appropriate caution should be practiced. For example, if an officer or victim inadvertently rubs across the surface where a latent print is located, the simple movement across the latent can render the print useless. Another enemy of the latent fingerprint is moisture. Appropriate caution should be observed by both the officer and the victim.

5.2 *Fingerprint categories*

Fingerprints are generally classified into four categories: latent, known or inked, plastic, and patent prints. With the exception of known prints, latent prints are by far the most common category (Figure 5.1). Fingerprints found at crime scenes are generally termed "latent prints" or "prints" regardless of the category to which they belong. **Latent** means hidden. This means that, before the prints can be seen, they need to be developed with the use of chemical or lighting enhancement. Although not always hidden, latent prints can most often be readily observed by simply using oblique or reflective lighting onto the surface where the latent might be located. The item can then be preserved accordingly and processed by the officer or by the investigative unit assigned such duty.

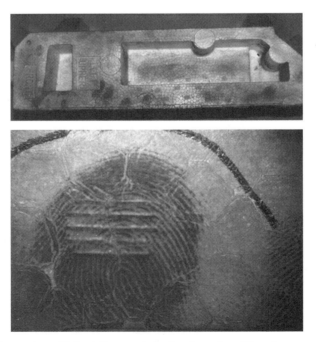

Figure 5.1 - Examples of latent fingerprints developed on Styrofoam packaging

Known fingerprints, or inked prints, are those prints taken at the time of arrest or booking, or ones taken by the investigator from a known person that can be documented, these are sometimes called elimination prints.

Plastic prints are those that can be seen on a surface such as putty or other such soft surface and need not be enhanced through chemical or lighting methods. These prints can easily be memorialized through photography. Better still, if the item onto which the print is located can be removed and booked into police property, that is the better course of action.

Patent prints are those that have been deposited via some type of oil, blood, or other fluid, which again are visible and need no enhancement. These types of prints have used material other than perspiration as a transfer medium to register the prints.

5.3 Latent fingerprints

Whether the first unit responder is at a major or non-major crime scene, the potential for there being fingerprints is quite substantial. Therefore, the officer should be ever vigilant to give particular attention to the types of questions asked of a victim and/or witness and the type of preliminary investigation that will be carried out. It is important for officers to realize that in determining whether there are fingerprints present, they need to look at potential surfaces where latent prints might have been deposited, rather than looking for the fingerprints themselves. Many times, to the untrained eye, what appear to be fingerprints are simply smudges. That is not to say that officers should ignore that particular item or surface, but rather that they should approach the situation cautiously. The surface in question might contain other latent fingerprints that the officer cannot see and if they are ignored, potential evidence could be lost. True latent prints must be developed through the use of chemical enhancements (covered later in the chapter) to allow the officer to better understand the potential of latents. What makes fingerprints unique in their usefulness as evidence is to realize that a complete latent print is not required for identification purposes, however, a complete latent is always preferable. But, most of the time, identifications are effected with partial latent prints.

Latent prints can be said to be identifiable, usable, of AFIS or non-AFIS quality. A latent print is considered **identifiable** when that print can be compared and matched to a specific person to the exclusion of all others. A latent print is considered **usable** when it can be used for elimination purposes, but not necessarily for identification purposes. For example, a print is usable when, although specific identification information such as ridge characteristics cannot be distinguished, pattern type can be. Any subsequent comparisons can then eliminate potential suspects, but cannot identify a specific suspect. A latent print is considered **AFIS quality** when that print is such that it can be entered into the automated fingerprint system (the fingerprint computer) and results can be produced. A print is considered **non-AFIS** quality if the print is of insufficient quality to enter into the fingerprint computer. The latent fingerprint can still be identifiable, but not

of AFIS quality. Why is it important for the first unit responder to have an understanding of whether a print is usable or identifiable? Simply so that the officer knows the significance of the potential evidence and does not turn a blind eye.

Determining whether there are latent prints is not complicated. The officer needs simply to ask a few questions and, where possible, do a walk-through of the crime scene with the victim or witnesses, explaining the need for potential items that might contain latent prints. Simple questions such as: "What appears out of place?" "Are there drawers that have been opened and rifled through?" "What items were taken?" Not extremely in-depth questions, but enough to establish possible areas in which latent prints might be present. Where the victim or another person familiar with the premises is not present, the officer should defer doing a walk-through. The officer should conspicuously place a handwritten note at a place where anyone entering the premises will see the note, not unduly disturb any potential evidence, and immediately contact the local agency to do a walk-through of the premises. Should officers give up in their quest for latent prints if victims or witnesses state that they think the suspect was wearing gloves? The answer is an unequivocal no. Where certain items have been discovered by the suspect(s) and they want to examine the item more closely, oftentimes they will remove their gloves temporarily. During those moments, the like-lihood of leaving prints is quite high. As an example, there have been numer-ous cases where suspects left glove impressions throughout a scene, and, when a gun (or jewelry) was found, the gloves were temporarily removed during inspection, allowing the deposit of latent prints that were subse-quently developed and later identified. Even in those instances where gloves or other hand coverings are found, the officer is reminded to use diligence while conducting the preliminary investigation. From personal experience, I have found that the type of gloves worn can have an impact on the case. For example, suspects simply assume that if they are wearing gloves, they will not leave fingerprints. Not so. Thin, medical-type gloves in some instances have not afforded protection to the criminal suspects who were using them. Because of the heat and amount of perspiration produced by the criminal suspect(s), the finger impression went through the gloves and onto the surfaces that were being touched by the suspects. (I have personally made a few identifications in just such cases.) Where gloves have been used, the first unit responder should make note of this and have the scene pro-cessed, passing along the glove information to investigators. There are situ-ations where glove prints can be used for identification purposes, as some types of gloves will leave their own unique impressions at the scene. Can latent prints be developed from the inside of gloves? The answer, theoreti-cally, is yes. Theoretically, anything is possible. But the probability of devel-oping usable prints is extremely low, let alone identifiable prints. However, gloves found at the scene of a crime should never be discarded. To the contrary, gloves are evidence and should be treated as such.

What about those instances where another type of hand covering was found at the scene, such as socks, towels, and the like? In those instances, the officer should still process or have the scene processed because of the major importance of the point of entry (POE). In situations where hand covering is found at or near the point of exit, the officer needs to be concerned with preserving the POE. At that point, the likelihood of the suspect's wearing gloves was very slim, if at all. Generally speaking, to break into a dwelling, a locked room, or a strong container, a significant amount of force must be used. The more force used to gain entry, the greater the likelihood that more energy was used by the suspect. When more energy is used, the greater the metabolic rate of the perpetrator; hence, the greater the chances of latent fingerprints being present. True latent prints are, in reality, nothing more than the moisture of suspects being exuded through the pores of their fingers, palms, and bottoms of toes and feet. Again, the greater the metabolic rate, the greater the probability of latents being present. In order for latent prints to be present, a transfer medium such as perspiration or other substance must be on the surface of the hands or feet. One can liken a fingerprint to a stamp being dipped into ink. The transfer medium is the ink and the impression made by the stamping template is simply the result of the ink being transferred onto the item that the stamp comes into contact with. Should the hand be moved during the contact or deposit of a latent fingerprint, just as in an inked stamp, there will appear a smear. However, this should not deter the officer from seeking out those surfaces that might contain latent fingerprints.

Generally speaking, the best items for the presence of latent prints are those that have smooth, glossy surfaces. However, the officer should not discount any other type of surface simply because it is not smooth and glossy. As stated before, latent prints can be anywhere. There are a myriad of processes that can be used to develop latent fingerprints on many different surfaces. The most common form of latent fingerprint development is one with which all officers should be familiar: brush and powder. To assist the officer in better understanding the many processes, a list of methods with the reaction and type of surface best suited for each is shown in Figure 5.2.

At this point a word, of caution is in order. Officers should not become frustrated when latent fingerprints do not develop. As stated earlier, latent prints depend on the transfer medium being present for latent prints to be present. If there is no transfer medium, there will be no latents. Officers should also be aware, to hold down the frustration rate, although suspects might not have been wearing gloves, there is still the distinct possibility that latent prints were not left. How does this occur? The moist hand might be depositing prints at the POE and, as the suspect(s) continues to touch things throughout the crime scene, the hands can become dry. Unless there is that transfer medium present, the likelihood of there being latents is basically slim to none. There is still the possibility of plastic prints or patent prints being present at the crime scene. In many instances, unfortunately, the officer who does not locate possible items containing latent prints will sometimes cut short the initial investigation and interview. The necessity of a good, thorough, preliminary investigation being conducted by the first unit responder cannot be over emphasized. It cannot be said too often that, it is always better to get too much than not enough. Even the most experienced officer has at one time or another overlooked the possibility of plastic or patent prints being present at a crime scene.

Plastic or patent prints are generally much easier to locate than latent prints, due to their visibility. Officers locating these types of prints should note and preserve the surfaces where the prints are located. At a minimum, these prints can be photographed without a great deal of difficulty. For those agencies where patrol personnel will be collecting these types of prints, the process is relatively simple. Photograph the prints (with a scale), and then collect the item(s) to where the prints are located. In some instances, a plastic print can be collected through a mold of the print. In other situations, a patent print can be lifted in the same manner as a latent. A word of caution: always err on the side of safely obtaining the fingerprint. This means choose the best course of action that will allow the investigator to collect the evidence possible to build the case. The first unit responder will be most responsible for the identifying the location, documentation, and preservation of latent fingerprints until such time as the latent print will be developed and collected.

METHOD	SURFACES APPLICABLE
Physical powder dusting	Smooth, nonporous surfaces
Brush and powder	Some semiporous surfaces
Magnetic powder	
Ninhydrin	Paper, cardboard
DFO	Paper, cardboard
Physical developer	Paper, cardboard
Silver nitrate	Paper, cardboard
Laser/Alternate light source (ALS)	Smooth, non- or slightly porous surfaces
Cyanoacrylate ester (super glue)	Plastic, metal, glass, glossy surfaces
Gentian (crystal) violet	Tapes, adhesive/electrical
Sticky Side powder ®	All types of tapes (Sticky Side)
Small particle reagent (SPR)	Sticky or wet surfaces, concrete
Oblique lighting	Smooth and surfaces that do not reflect

Figure 5.2 - Methods by which fingerprints can be developed and visualized.

5.4 *Review*

The types of fingerprints and the types of surfaces on which fingerprints will commonly be found were discussed in this chapter. Remember to try to contact someone who is familiar with the environment to do a walk-through with the officer. Since the victim has been traumatized, care and sympathy should be extended during the interview and walk-through to determine where the evidence might be. Where the items can be set aside to prevent contamination or further distress to the victim, this action is advisable. The type of surface is more critical in determining if there is a possibility of latent prints rather than seeing the latent prints themselves on an item. Latent prints cannot always be seen without the aid of enhancers. Some types of fingerprints can be seen without the use of enhancers, such as plastic and patent prints. These types of prints will be much more easily detected.

The four types of fingerprints are **latent, known, plastic**, and **patent**. Of those types of fingerprints developed or detected at crime scenes, the prints will be either **identifiable** or **usable**. Taken a step further, those agencies that possess an Automated Fingerprint Identification System (or AFIS) will make a determination if the latent prints developed are of AFIS or non-AFIS quality and process them accordingly.

Criminal suspects might not leave latent fingerprints at a crime although they were not wearing gloves. In order to leave prints, there must be a transfer medium present. The first unit responder should also be ever mindful to determine if gloves were worn or if hand covering in the form of socks or other cloth obtained at the residence was used. If the hand covering was obtained at the premises, then protection of the POE should be given priority.

Latent fingerprints as a form of physical evidence are excellent. However, realistically, fewer than 50% of the attempts result in developing latent fingerprints. This should not deter the first officer on the scene from taking the necessary precautions. As the old adage goes: always plan for the best, but expect the worst. Officers should enter a crime scene with an open mind in hopes of retrieving latent fingerprints and other forms of physical evidence, and not until the contrary is demonstrated should the officer give up hope.

5.5 Test questions

T   F   1. Latent fingerprints will be left at crime scenes by suspects who do not wear gloves.

T   F   2. Generally speaking, the most important area of concentration for latent fingerprint evidence is the point of entry.

T   F   3. Victims and witnesses will always be forthcoming with information and might even volunteer information to the first unit responder.

T   F   4. In an instance where the victim was adamant that a suspect was wearing gloves, officers should not concern themselves with the presence of latent prints.

T   F   5. Where the officer observes gloves or other hand covering at the point of exit, the officer should disregard the evidence and request the victim to dispose of the gloves or other hand covering.

T   F   6. A partial latent print is of no value for purposes of identification.

T   F   7. Glove prints are of little value at the crime scene.

T   F   8. While doing a walk-through of the premises, the officer observes nothing out of place. The officer should infer that the suspect(s) did not examine that area for valuables.

T   F   9. Special attention should be given to small jewelry-type boxes and places where firearms may have been located.

T   F   10. A partial latent print can be just as powerful as a complete latent print for proving or disproving identification.

T   F   11. A latent print that is not identifiable is of no value to the investigation.

5.6 *Answers*

1. **FALSE**   For latent prints to be left at a scene, there must be a transfer medium on the hands of the suspect. If the hands are dry, even without hand covering, the likelihood of there being latent prints is extremely remote.

2. **TRUE**   This is the area in which the suspect is usually doing the perspiring and, as such, the likelihood of there being latent prints present is greatly increased.

3. **FALSE**   Victims and witnesses have been traumatized and need to be asked direct questions to elicit the correct answers for the investigation. Many times, the victims or witnesses do not volunteer information, not because they don't want to, but because they haven't thought about it or may feel the information is not pertinent.

4. **FALSE**   Glove patterns, in some instances, are very unique and can be identified. Suspects may also remove their gloves when examining particular objects like guns or jewelry and forget to put their gloves back on immediately thereafter.

5. **FALSE**   Although the presence of gloves can create frustration on the part of the officer, gloves are still evidence and should be handled and preserved as such.

6. **FALSE**   A partial latent print is just as important as a complete latent print. A partial latent can be identified just as effectively as a complete latent.

7. **FALSE**   See Answers #4 and #5. Glove prints are evidence and should be treated as evidence in the case.

8. **FALSE**   The officer doing a walk-through of the scene should always keep an open mind. The purpose of doing a walk-through with someone familiar with the premises is to determine what is out of place and which items might contain latent fingerprints.

9. **TRUE**   Small containers and places where firearms may have been located might yield latent prints, as the suspect(s) in many instances could have removed their gloves to examine the items.

10. **TRUE**   See answer to #6.

11. **FALSE**   Although a latent print may not be identifiable, the print can still be used for purposes of elimination. Thus, the value is just as great to disprove who committed the crime as would be to prove who committed the crime.

chapter six

Case preparation/ courtroom testimony

Before any criminal case is brought before a grand jury, judge (preliminary hearing), or petit jury for presentation, the necessity for proper preparation is critical. The officer who was the first unit responder will need to prepare just as much, if not more, than the Assistant District Attorney (ADA)who will be presenting the case. This means that these officers must take the necessary safeguards to ensure that they are intimately familiar with the case. Intimately familiar does not simply mean relying on memory alone to recall the facts and events that took place on the date of the crime. All actions taken and any supplemental reports that were generated by the officer should be reviewed. Any notes, such as a sketch, statements by witnesses, victims, or suspects, that were recorded should be reviewed by the officer. Any evidence that the officer identified, collected, or booked should be reviewed. The review of the evidence should be done well in advance of the officer's appearance.

6.1 Case review by officer

The review process undertaken by the officer is not something that should be done alone. Case preparation needs to be done in conjunction with the ADA who will be presenting the case. The reason is straightforward; the ADA should walk the officer through the questioning that will occur during the **direct** examination (giving testimony for the side that subpoenaed the witness; or, as in the case where both sides subpoena the officer, the side that first calls the officer as a witness) or the people's presentation. For the ADA to properly establish a line of questioning, he or she should have more than simply reports. This preparation phase is commonly called a DA conference or pretrial conference. This facet of the case is the most critical. It is at this point that the ADA establishes how the case will proceed. It is also during this phase, case preparation, that the ADA now has, or should have, some idea or can speculate on what the defense might be as evidence in the case has been given to the defense attorney under the rules of discovery (turning over to the other side all evidence that is planned to be presented during the hearing or trial). At this point, should officers feel something is not right with the case or evidence, they speak up. The ADA can make quick alterations at this point. It is not wise to wait for the case to get into court before any questions or concerns about the case are raised. Damage control is more easily accomplished prior to trial than in the courtroom.

Generally, it is the defense who will most benefit from discovery. Discovery includes photos, written statements, sketches, notes, and lists of potential witnesses. Oftentimes, unless a case is set to go to trial, ADAs are somewhat difficult to contact. Because of case loads, especially in more-populated jurisdictions, ADAs, will devote appropriate time to conducting a case preparation interview with the officer prior to appearing in court. Preliminary hearings are done for the purpose of establishing probable/sufficient cause to bind a criminal defendant over for trial. This often means the barest of evidence need only be presented by the ADA to get a holding by the judge. The action on the part of the ADA does not relieve the officer from still making the attempt to setup a conference or interview with the ADA. A conscientious officer will always make the attempt to contact the ADA despite a history of disappointments.

Another very important facet of preparation that needs to be addressed is dress and appearance. How the officer appears in court will have a greater impact than the officer often realizes. The appearance of the officer establishes credibility in the eyes of the judge or the jury and, in some instances, will have just as substantial an impact as the evidence in the case. When the officer is dressed in casual attire, the message is that the officer appears to have a casual attitude about the case and the court process. First impressions last forever. The officer needs to keep this advice in mind and establish credibility and professionalism from the outset. Appropriate attire is generally considered to be a conservative suit, sport coat/blazer and trousers, or dress uniform. This attire should never deviate when appearing in court, as the officer's line of work should never be considered anything less than a profession.

6.2 Courtroom procedure

During an appearance in court, the officer will be subject to a series of phases during the session. The phases consist of the introduction, the body of the questions and admission of evidence, and a follow-up or rebuttal. The people will present their side of the case first, then the defense; then the rebuttal will be made, again by prosecution first, then by the defense. Prior to being called as a witness to testify, the officer might have to wait outside the courtroom. A word of caution is offered at this point: If the jurisdiction where the officer will be testifying does not have a waiting room devoted strictly to law enforcement, the officer will probably be required to wait outside the courtroom until called to testify. Officers should realize that while waiting, they are being observed. The observation might be by potential witnesses, by potential jurors, or even by a defense attorney. Officers should keep in mind that maintaining a professional demeanor is the order of the day. They should refrain from speaking to anyone but the ADA about the case until called as a witness. Once called, the introduction phase has begun.

6.2.1 Introduction phase

During the introduction phase of the proceedings, the officer, for the most part, will be introduced to the court, the court attaché, the defendant, and, in the case of a jury trial, the jury via questioning. It is at this point that the credentials of the officer will be established by the ADA. The officer can expect opening questions such as: Could you state your name and spell your last name for the record? By whom are you employed? How long have you been employed? What is your present assignment? Do you have any special training? This stage is sometimes called a **shallow voir dire**, although in its truest sense, expert witnesses are *voir dired* to establish their knowledge and expertise. Experts can also render opinions, which generally, first unit responders will not.

6.2.2 Direct/cross examination phase

The next phase, the body of questions or direct examination, is to determine what the officer has done or observed, and any other actions the officer may have taken in the case. It is during this phase of questioning that the officer should testify in a fashion that will be credible, not overpowering, and in language the court or jury can understand. The officer should refrain from using slang or jargon, such as radio or penal-code sections when answering questions or providing explanations, unless to qualify an answer. Although officers are, in fact, agents of the government, they need to testify in a fashion that appears as neutral as possible.

Testimony is based on the facts and evidence of the case. Generally, most questions will be asked in such a way as to elicit a yes or no answer. Where a question is asked of the officer for which the attorney wants a yes or no answer and the officer cannot answer yes or no, the officer should say so. Tell the questioning attorney that the answer is not simply yes or no, but that it must be qualified. Although not an expert witness, the officer certainly has the ability to qualify any response to a question should the need arise. Should there be a challenge on the part of the attorney, officers can turn to the judge to make their request. It is during this direct questioning that most of the evidence will be introduced by the prosecution. Officers, when asked about certain actions or pieces of evidence that they booked, should answer directly. The officer should also listen to the question, think about it, and then give the appropriate response. The officer who has difficulty testifying is one who anticipates the content of the questioning by either attorney. Officers should refrain from anticipating the meaning of a question, what the attorney is trying to do, or where the attorney is trying to go with a particular line of questioning. Should the officer experience frustration at the line of questioning by the attorneys, the officer should remain calm and not become visibly frustrated. (e.g., rolling one's eyes after the question is asked, or letting out a big sigh, or peering at the questioning attorney). If officers do not understand the question, they should ask the attorney to repeat the question, or respond with "I don't quite understand. Could you rephrase the question?" Do not become visibly shaken. Remember, you are being observed and what you say, how you say it, and your appearance and demeanor will have an impact on the believability or credibility of your testimony. Nervousness is a part of the process of testifying. There is probably no one—from the newly appointed officer to the veteran officer—who is without some type of nervousness when testifying. Quite frankly, after 25 years of testifying, I still become a little nervous at times. If that nervousness is to the point where one's mouth is dry and speaking is difficult, do not be afraid to ask for a drink of water. This not only calms the officer, but it also serves to slow the proceedings, which usually will allow all sides to compose themselves and their thoughts.

When the direct examination is complete, the opposing attorney will begin the cross-examination process. This process allows the opposing attorney to clarify any issues or questions that were opened or raised in the direct examination phase. Much of the process of the cross-examination will be the same as direct examination. Similar questions will be asked and, in some instances, it may sound to the officer that the same questions are being asked. If that is the case, the officer should look to the ADA in case there is an objection to the particular line of questioning. If an objection is made to a particular question, the officer should immediately stop speaking until the matter is resolved by the court. If the objection is sustained (meaning that the court finds in favor of the objection), the officer is not required to continue answering the question. If the objection is overruled (meaning the court does not find in favor of the objection) the officer must answer the question. If officers have forgotten the question, they should say so. State to the questioning attorney: "Could you repeat the question?" Then, of course, give the appropriate response.

6.2.3 Closing phase

The third phase, the rebuttal, is the phase that allows both sides to clarify issues that were made during the direct- and cross-examination phase of the testimony. Should there be issues concerning the evidence, records, notes, etc., the rebuttal phase is meant to clarify any misunderstandings—although it is sometimes said that the court process is still difficult to understand, even after all phases have been undertaken. The officer should give the same attention to detail, neutrality, and demeanor during this final phase as was given during the direct and cross-examinations. Most often, the testimony of the officer will be less than 1 hour. However, there are those instances in the more complex cases where an officer may be on the witness stand for hours or even days. It is trying for officers, but they should not lose composure in spite of having to endure long testimony. Should the appearance of officers require more than 1 day of testimony, they should again keep in mind their appearance and demeanor. It should go without saying, but needs to be mentioned, DO NOT wear the same clothing two days in a row. Some would say it really makes no difference. Officers should always maintain the perspective that someone, the judge or jury, will notice and that will affect their credibility. As stated before, officers are testifying as professionals and nothing should be done to bring about a less than professional perspective about their testimony.

In countries other than the United States where an officer might be required to testify, the process of presenting a case might differ slightly or a great deal. However, the fundamentals or the basics on the part of the officer should remain the same: proper case preparation through thorough familiarization with the facts and evidence of the case and presenting oneself in a professional manner. In other countries, the officer needs to act according to the laws and protocol of that country, and not make assumptions or presumptions about how a case will proceed.

6.2.4 Follow-up by the officer

Upon completion of their testimony, officers need to follow up with the prosecutor for several reasons: to obtain the outcome of the case, to determine the credibility and/or believability of the officers, and how they might improve future appearances. Officers should also solicit any suggestions from the prosecutor on how they might better present their portion of the case in the future and determine what, if anything, they did incorrectly. Testifying in court is not an easy undertaking but one that is necessary to present a case against a criminal defendant. Officers should not take this obligation lightly because, when the obligation is not taken seriously, cases are lost or officers are embarrassed on the stand in front of the judge or jury. Certainly, no one—except maybe the defense—wants to see this happen. Proper preparation is the key to the successful presentation of anything. When proper preparation fails, so does the ensuing case.

6.3 Review

In this chapter, the preparation and courtroom testimony were discussed. The varied aspects of case presentation necessitate that the officer always properly prepare with the ADA for giving testimony. The officer should be given direction by the ADA as to how the questioning and introduction of the evidence will proceed. A walk-through or dry run of questioning should be undertaken by the ADA with the officer.

While giving testimony, officers will be questioned about their qualifications, experience, observations, and actions regarding the case. The officer while testifying should remain calm, qualify an answer if the need arises, and not appear to be prejudicial regarding the case, the defendant, or the attorneys. Courtroom demeanor is very important.

Proper courtroom attire can be just as important as the evidence. A casual appearance might be mistaken as a casual attitude toward the case. Credibility is the key to successful testimony. Although testifying as an agent of the government, the officer wants to appear neutral, present a professional demeanor, and project the knowledge of the case that is expected. The officer will be subjected to direct examination as well as cross-examination. They should not try to second-guess where the questioning is going or what is trying to be established. The officer should maintain a high degree of professionalism, whether being questioned by the prosecution or the defense. While giving testimony, the officer should refrain from using slang or jargon to describe actions in the case.

As with all aspects of life, one strives to continually improve. Regarding courtroom testimony, the follow-up with the ADA and with peers regarding testimony will improve the ability of the officer to better testify in future cases. Upon completion of giving testimony, the officer should always evaluate what could have been done better and implement that lesson in future cases; that is the mark of a true professional.

6.4 Test questions

T   F   1. When testifying, although notes are permissible, the officer should rely on memory to recall the events of the case.

T   F   2. The ADA should never review an officer's testimony before courtroom presentation as that is considered improper.

T   F   3. A good ADA will use only reports produced by the investigation and initial responder to build a criminal case.

T   F   4. If the officer feels something is wrong with the case or has concerns about a certain facet of the case, those concerns should wait until the case is being presented in court.

T   F   5. When being questioned by either side, the officer should try to anticipate the meaning or direction of the line of questioning.

T   F   6. Court appearance and demeanor have little to do with the credibility of the witness.

T   F   7. Because first unit responders are not expert witnesses, they should not qualify an answer. They must always answer yes or no.

                 8. Being questioned in court about an officer's credentials, experience, and knowledge is known as _____ _____.

9. Questioning by the side that subpoenaed the witness is known as_____ examination.

10. Questioning by the other side is known as _____ examination.

11. Giving the other side all evidence that is intended to be presented in court, including names of potential witnesses, is known as _____.

12. If an objection is made on an issue by either side and the judge directs the witness to answer the question, the objection has been _____.

6.5 Test answers

1. **FALSE** Officers should not rely on memory alone. They should ask to review notes and reports when they are unsure and need to refresh their memory.

2. **FALSE** Only the most inexperienced ADA would not want to have a conference with the officer to prepare the officer as to what type of questions might be asked in court.

3. **FALSE** Any ADA would be remiss if he/she did not use more than reports and the investigation to build a criminal case. There is the evidence, the officer's own feelings about the case, and the defendant to consider as well.

4. **FALSE** The time to bring up concerns about the case, good or bad, are before the courtroom presentation. It is much easier to prevent something than to repair the damage.

5. **FALSE** Although officers are governmental agents, their testimony should be neutral. In addition, officers trying to anticipate the content of the question or where the questioning is going, they might fail to fully understand the question and not answer the question to the best of their ability.

6. **FALSE** First impressions last forever. Credibility, appearance, and demeanor go hand in hand in convincing a judge or jury that officers know what they are testifying to and that they have veracity. A casual appearance can have a negative effect.

7. **FALSE** Just because the officer is not an expert witness does not mean the officer cannot qualify answers if the need arises. Although

not entitled to render an opinion like an expert witness, the ability to qualify an answer certainly falls within the purview of the officer.

8.   Officers being questioned in court about their credentials, experience, and knowledge are known as *voir dire*.

9.   Questioning by the side who subpoenaed the witness is known as *direct* examination.

10.   Questioning by the other side is known as *cross-examination*.

11.   Giving the other side all evidence that is intended to be presented in court, including names of potential witnesses, is known as *discovery*.

12.   If an objection is made on an issue by either side and the judge directs the witness to answer the question, the objection has been *overruled*.

appendix

Items and evidence encountered by the first unit responder

The following photographs depict examples of many of the most commonly encountered items and types of evidence the first unit responder might discover. The examples are meant to serve as a tool of awareness for the first unit responder. The photos are intended to demonstrate the following:

1. The many types of potential evidence
2. The types of evidence and surfaces that might yield latent fingerprints
3. An example of a completed comparison of latent to known fingerprints

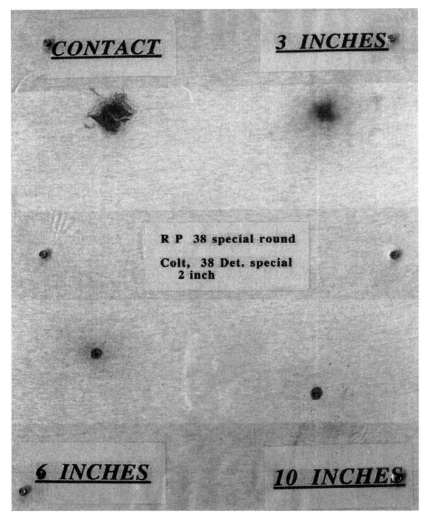

Figure A.1   To assist the first unit responder in understanding gunshot damage to clothing, this illustration shows four distances from which a gunshot is fired and the damage done. The weapon was a 38 spec. cal., 2" Colt revolver. (Display courtesy of Off. Ralph Schoenstein)

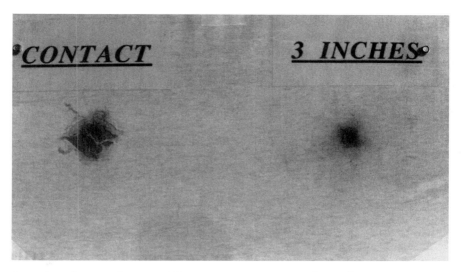

Figure A.2 This is a close-up of the damage done by gunshots. The damage done by a contact shot and 3″ shot to material is substantial. There are also powder burns present.

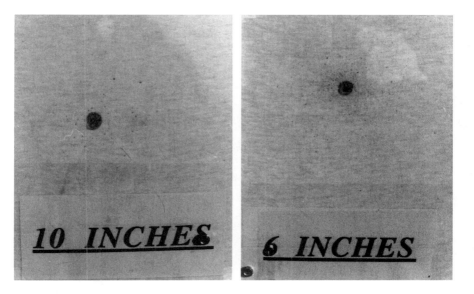

Figure A.3 This figure shows the lessening of damage as the distance increases from where the shot is fired. Both 6″ and 10″ show substantially less damage although there are more powder specks. The holes also appear more symmetrical.

Figure A.4 This figure illustrates the side of a vehicle that was fired upon by police personnel with 40-caliber handguns. The enormity of the holes shows the power of the 40-caliber round.

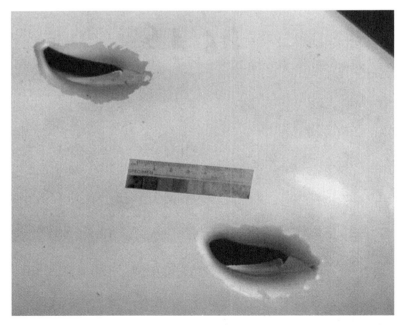

Figure A.5 A close-up of the elongated bullet holes from police weapons shows the enormity of force as well as indicating the shots were fired from angles. The key-holing effect of the bullets is characteristic of angled shots.

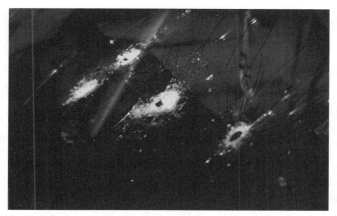

Figure A.6 This figure shows how exit holes from bullets quite often leave what is called a bell characteristic on the side from which the bullets exit. The spider webbing in the window can sometimes be used to determine which shots were fired first. However, in automobile glass, due to the layers and the elasticity of the glass, inaccurate assumptions can easily be made.

Figure A.7 These are examples of a bullet's exit from a vehicle's front window. The glass that is pushed up, the cone, shows how elastic automobile glass is.

Figure A.8 This view is from inside the vehicle outward, following the path of the bullets.

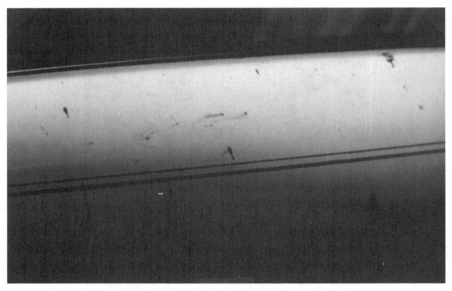

Figure A.9 This figure shows how blood patterns can indicate from which direction it was shed. Notice the tails on the blood. Tails show the direction from which the blood was shed and in which it is traveling.

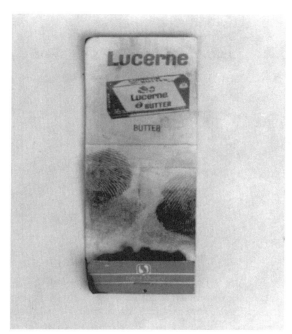

Figure A.10 This is an example of what many first unit responders will encounter when responding to a crime. A simple matchbook that has been discarded by a suspect might contain very incriminating evidence, such as fingerprints. Small objects must not be overlooked.

Figure A.11 This example shows a close-up of the evidence contained on the matchbook. Although the latent fingerprint is a partial print, it is good enough for identification purposes.

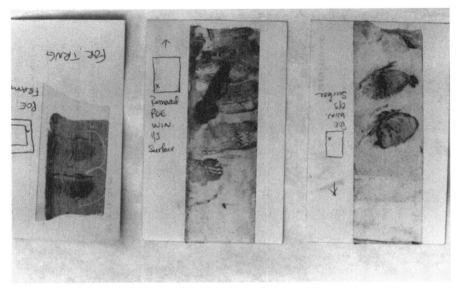

Figure A.12 This figure shows something that all first unit responders will encounter in their career: glove prints. There are three different types of glove prints included in this figure.

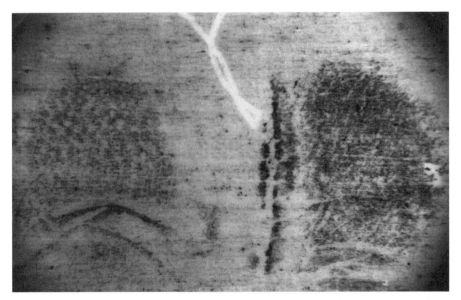

Figure A.13 This is a close-up of a set of glove prints contained in figure A.12. Glove prints should not be a cause for frustration. The investigation should be completed before a conclusion is reached.

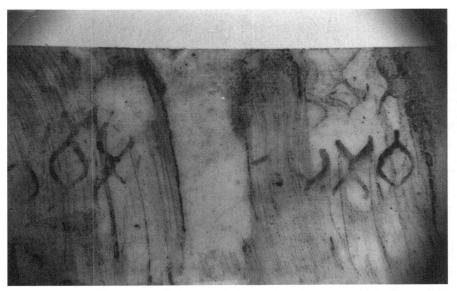

Figure A.14 A close-up of a different set of glove prints demonstrated in Figure A.12. These prints are representative of the rubber Playtex type of glove.

Figure A.15 This figure demonstrates the resulting deformations of bullets after they have been fired and have hit an object.

Figure A.16 A close-up of one of the expended bullets in Figure A.15. The mushroom effect is quite common.

Figure A.17 This figure shows three casings together. Notice at the base that the casings are different. The difference allows the officer to determine what type of weapon was used—revolver or semi-automatic—simply by sight. (The two outside casings are from semi-automatic guns. The center casing is from a revolver.)

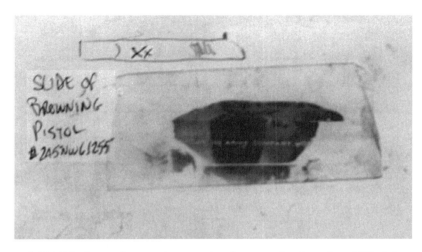

Figure A.18 This figure shows a latent print that was developed and lifted from the side of a slide from a semi-automatic weapon.

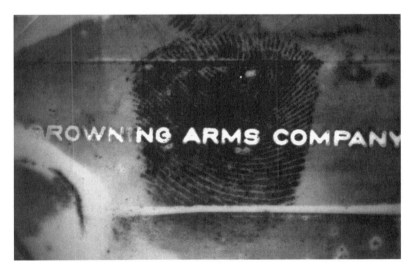

Figure A.19 This figure shows a close-up of the print appearing in Figure A.18. As observed, the print is usable and identifiable. (Remember, however, the likelihood of obtaining good, usable prints from firearms is usually quite low, so take great care to properly handle guns that will be processed for latent prints.)

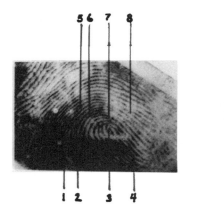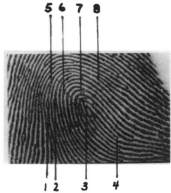

Figure A.20 An example of an identification chart, or what is commonly known as charting. When a latent print is developed and is of sufficient quality, a demo chart can be prepared. The eight "points" are not the only factors in considering the identification. The pattern type and the relationship of the points are critical in the identification process as well.

Figure A.21 An example of one of the most commonly used methods to gain entry into a dwelling—smashing a window in a front or side door.

bibliography

Bennett, W. and Hess, K.M. *Criminal Investigation*, (5th ed.). Belmont, CA: Wadsworth, 1998.

Cowger, J.E. *Friction Ridge Skin Comparison and Identification of Fingerprints.* New York: Elsevier Science, 1983.

Fisher, B.A.J. *Techniques of Crime Scene Investigation*, (5th ed.). Boca Raton, FL: CRC, 1993.

Federal Bureau of Investigation. *The Science of Fingerprints.* U.S. Government, Washington, D.C., 1984.

Federal Bureau of Investigation. *Handbook of Forensic Science.* U.S. Government, Washington, D.C., 1995.

Geberth, V.J. *Practical Homicide Investigation Tactics, Procedures and Forensic Techniques,* (2nd ed.). New York: Elsevier Science, 1990.

Hazelwood, R.R., and Burgess, A.W. *Practical Aspects of Rape Investigation A Multidisciplinary Approach.* New York: Elsevier Science, 1987.

Lee, H.C. and Gaensslen, R.E. *Advances in Fingerprint Technology.* Boca Raton, FL: CRC, 1994.

Lee, H. C. (Ed.). *Crime Scene Investigation.* Taiwan: Central Police University Press, 1994.

Mac Donald, H. *Blood Spatter Interpretation.* Corning, NY: Laboratory of Forensic Science, 1982.

Margot, P. and Leonard, C. *Fingerprint Detection Techniques,* (6th ed.). Lausanne: Université de Lausanne, 1994.

Masters, N.E. *Safety for the Forensic Indentification Specialist,* Salem, OR: Lightning Powder Co., 1995.

Menzel, R.E. *Fingerprint Detection with Lasers.* New York: Marcell Dekker, 1980.

Moenssens, A.A., Starrs, J.E., Henderson, C.E., and Inbau, Fred E. *Scientific Evidence in Civil & Criminal Cases,* (4th ed.). Westbury, NY: The Fountain Press, 1995.

Ogle, R.R. *Crime Scene Investigation and Physical Evidence Manual.* 1992.

Olsen, R.D., Sr. *Scott's Fingerprint Mechanics,* Springfield, IL: Charles C Thomas, 1978.

Reynerson, J.M. and Chisum, W.J. *Evidence and Crime Scene Reconstruction,* (3rd ed.). Redding, CA: Reynerson. 1992.

Saferstein, R. *Criminalistics,* (6th ed.). Upper Saddle River, NJ: Prentice-Hall, 1998.

Saferstein, R. *Forensic Science Handbook,* Vol. I, II, III. Englewood Cliffs, NJ: Prentice-Hall, 1988.

Tuthill, H. *Individualization: Principles and Procedures in Criminalistics.* Salem, OR: Lightning Powder Co., 1994.

Index